DK EYEWITNESS TRAVEL

TOP 10
PRAGUE

THEODORE SCHWINKE

Penguin
Random
House

Top 10 Prague Highlights

Welcome to Prague **5**

Exploring Prague **6**

Prague Highlights.......................**10**

Prague Castle **12**

St Vitus Cathedral.......................**16**

Old Town Square.........................**18**

Charles Bridge **22**

The Loreto **26**

Old Jewish Cemetery..................**28**

Trade Fair Palace........................**32**

Convent of St Agnes....................**34**

Wenceslas Square **36**

Petřín Hill **38**

The Top 10 of Everything

Moments in History **42**

Writers and Composers..............**44**

Museums and Galleries **46**

Places of Worship **48**

Communist Monuments **50**

Parks and Gardens......................**52**

House Signs **54**

Off the Beaten Track...................**58**

Haunted Places............................**60**

Eccentric Prague **62**

Children's Attractions **64**

Performing Arts Venues..............**66**

Clubs...**68**

Restaurants..................................**70**

Prague Dishes.............................**72**

Bars and Kavárnas **74**

Shops and Markets......................**76**

Prague for Free...........................**78**

Festivals.......................................**80**

CONTENTS

Prague Area by Area

Old Town......................................**84**

Malá Strana................................**92**

Prague Castle and Hradčany....**100**

Josefov.......................................**108**

New Town...................................**114**

Greater Prague **122**

Streetsmart

Getting To and Around Prague...**132**

Practical Information **134**

Places to Stay............................**140**

General Index............................**148**

Acknowledgments....................**156**

Phrase Book...............................**159**

Front cover and spine Church of Our Lady before Týn and the Old Town at sunset
Back cover Church of St Lawrence on Petřín Hill with Prague blanketed in mist below
Title page The Astronomical Clock at the Old Town Hall, Old Town Square

Welcome to
Prague

The City of a Hundred Spires, with its medieval cityscape intact, continues to dazzle as it has for the better part of a millennium. The Old Town Hall's Astronomical Clock still chimes the hour as crowds cross the cobblestoned Charles Bridge under the gaze of the castle. With Eyewitness Top 10 Prague, this well-preserved city is yours to explore.

Praguers call their city Matka měst – the Mother of Cities – a reference to a time in the 14th century when Prague served as the capital of the Holy Roman Empire. Architectural treasures like **Prague Castle**, **St Vitus Cathedral** and **The Loreto** testify to that former grandeur. But Prague is more than pretty buildings. The city of Dvořák, Kafka, Bedřich Smetana and Václav Havel still throbs with culture, music, literature, theatre – and intrigue. All who visit are bewitched by the spires and the cobbles, the shadows and the tiny lanes of the most enchanting city in Central Europe.

And did we mention the beer? The Czech Republic prides itself as the home of the world's finest lager. What could be better than winding through the Baroque streetscape of **Malá Strana**, taking in the National Gallery's collection of modern art at the **Trade Fair Palace** and enjoying the green spaces of the **Wallenstein Garden** or **Petřín Hill** and then retiring to a traditional pub like **U Zlatého tygra** to digest it all over a mug of Pilsner Urquell or Staropramen?

Whether you're coming for a weekend or a week, our Top 10 guide is designed to bring together the best of everything that Prague has to offer, from the bustle of the **New Town** and the imperial flavour of **Hradčany** to the Gothic splendour of the **Old Town** and the understated grace of the former Jewish quarter of **Josefov**. There are useful tips throughout, from seeking out what's free to avoiding the crowds, plus eight easy-to-follow itineraries to help you visit a clutch of sights in a relatively short space of time. Add inspiring photography and detailed maps, and you've got the essential pocket-sized travel companion. **Enjoy the book and enjoy Prague**.

Clockwise from top: **Charles Bridge, Wenceslas Square, Spanish Synagogue, Wallenstein Garden, fresco at The Loreto, stained glass at St Vitus Cathedral, Old Town Square roofs**

Exploring Prague

There is a wealth of things to see and do in Prague. Whether you're here just for the weekend or have the luxury of a couple of extra days, these two- and four-day itineraries will help you to plan your time and make the most of your visit.

Charles Bridge links the Old Town and Malá Strana quarters of Prague.

Two Days in Prague

Day ❶
MORNING
Marvel at the **Old Town Square** (see pp18–21), taking in the Astronomical Clock. Ramble through the tiny lanes towards **Charles Bridge** (see pp22–3).

AFTERNOON
Meander through **Malá Strana** (see pp92–9), pausing at **St Nicholas's Church** (see p94). Hike up **Nerudova** (see p93) – note the house signs (see pp54–5) – to **Prague Castle** (see pp12–15), where you can tour the **Old Royal Palace** (see p14) and **St Vitus Cathedral** (see pp16–17).

Day ❷
MORNING
Begin at **Josefov** (see pp108–13) and the **Jewish Museum** (see p47). Don't miss the **Old Jewish Cemetery** (see pp28–31). The **Convent of St Agnes** (see pp34–5) nearby houses the National Gallery's medieval art.

AFTERNOON
Take in **Wenceslas Square** (see pp36–7), the heart of the **New Town** (see

Astronomical Clock

pp114–21). Admire the **National Museum** (see p118) before walking down Narodní towards the river to the **National Theatre** (see p66).

Four Days in Prague

Day ❶
MORNING
Visit the **Powder Gate** and **Municipal House** (see p85) before making your way to the **Old Town Square** (see pp18–21). Then stroll to **Charles Bridge** (see pp22–3).

AFTERNOON
Wander through **Malá Strana** (see pp92–9) via **Nerudova** (see p93) to **Prague Castle** (see pp12–15) and its **Old Royal Palace** (see p14), **St Vitus Cathedral** (see pp16–17) and Golden Lane.

Day ❷
MORNING
Spend time at the **Jewish Museum** (see p47), focusing on the **Old Jewish**

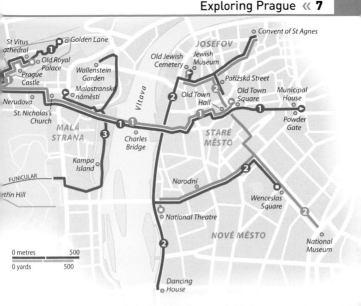

St Vitus Cathedral
Golden Lane
JOSEFOV
Convent of St Agnes
Old Royal Palace
Old Jewish Cemetery
Jewish Museum
Wallenstein Garden
Prague Castle
Malostranské náměstí
Vltava
Pařížská Street
Nerudova
Old Town Hall
Old Town Square
Municipal House
St. Nicholas's Church
MALÁ STRANA
Charles Bridge
STARÉ MĚSTO
Powder Gate
Kampa Island
FUNICULAR
etřín Hill
Narodní
Wenceslas Square
National Theatre
NOVÉ MĚSTO
National Museum

0 metres 500
0 yards 500

Dancing House

Key
— Two-day itinerary
— Four-day itinerary

The Wallenstein Garden is free for the public to enter, and hosts various cultural events during the summer.

Cemetery (see pp28–31). Explore exclusive Pařížská street then stop by the **Convent of St Agnes** (see pp34–5) for its collection of medieval art.

AFTERNOON
Head to the river and walk south along it to the **National Theatre** (see p66) and the **Dancing House** (see p116). Then take stately Narodní to **Wenceslas Square** (see pp36–7).

Day ❸
MORNING
Start at **Malostranské náměstí** (see p94). Amble through Malá Strana's green spaces, such as **Kampa Island** (see p52) and **Wallenstein Garden** (see p79). Make for **Petřín Hill** (see pp38–9) and ride the funicular up.

AFTERNOON
From Petřín, head to **Strahov Monastery** (see p38) and to **The Loreto** (see pp26–7). Be sure to stroll down tranquil **Nový Svět** (see p102).

Day ❹
MORNING
View the National Gallery's modern and contemporary art at the **Trade Fair Palace** (see pp32–3). Then check out **Výstaviště** and nearby **Stromovka** (see p124). From here it's a pleasant walk to **Prague Zoo** (see p123).

AFTERNOON
Explore **Vyšehrad**, the city's spiritual home (see p123). Be sure to visit the **Slavín Monument**, **Casemates** and **Sts Peter and Paul Cathedral** (see p127).

Top 10 Prague Highlights

Historic buildings in Prague's
Old Town Square

Prague Highlights	**10**	Old Jewish Cemetery	**28**
Prague Castle	**12**	Trade Fair Palace	**32**
St Vitus Cathedral	**16**	Convent of St Agnes	**34**
Old Town Square	**18**	Wenceslas Square	**36**
Charles Bridge	**22**	Petřín Hill	**38**
The Loreto	**26**		

TOP 10 Prague Highlights

At the heart of Europe, Prague's beautiful cityscape – from the Gothic exuberance of its castle and cathedral to the dignity of the medieval Jewish Cemetery and the 19th-century opulence of the "new" town – has been created and sustained by emperors, artists and religious communities. Under Communist rule, Prague was off the tourist map, but since 1989 the Czech capital has seen a surge of visitors eager to take in this spectacular city.

1 Prague Castle
Visitors can spend a day exploring this hilltop fortress of the Přemyslids, now home to the Czech president (see pp12–15).

St Vitus 2 Cathedral
The glory of the castle complex, St Vitus took nearly 600 years to build. Don't miss the exquisite stained glass and delightful gargoyles (see pp16–17).

3 Old Town Square
The city has few finer charms than watching the moon rise over the Old Town Square between the towers of the Church of Our Lady before Týn (see pp18–21).

The Loreto 5
Pilgrims have visited this Baroque shrine to the Virgin Mary since the 17th century. Visitors can admire the priceless ornaments held in its treasury (see pp26–7).

Charles Bridge 4
The huge crowds can make it hard to appreciate the beautiful statues on this bridge that links the city's two halves, but a visit is a must when in Prague (see pp22–3).

7 Trade Fair Palace

One of Europe's first Functionalist build-ings, the Trade Fair Palace now houses the National Gallery's collection of modern art *(see pp32–3)*.

6 Old Jewish Cemetery

This jumble of tombstones in the former Jewish ghetto gives little indication of the number of people buried here *(see pp28–31)*.

8 Convent of St Agnes

The oldest Gothic building in the city is now home to the National Gallery's collection of medieval art *(see pp34–5)*.

9 Wenceslas Square

From a humble horse market, the square has grown into a modern hub, with monuments recalling its role in the nation's history *(see pp36–7)*.

10 Petřín Hill

Perched above Malá Strana, the hill is crisscrossed with footpaths offering some of the city's best views. The Ukrainian church is wonderfully romantic *(see pp38–9)*.

🔟 ⭐ Prague Castle

Crowned by St Vitus Cathedral, Prague Castle *(Pražský hrad)* is the metaphorical and historical throne of the Czech lands. Around AD 880, Prince Bořivoj built a wooden fortress on this hilltop above the river, establishing it as the dynastic base of the Přemyslids. In the 14th century the castle became the seat of the Holy Roman Empire. Much of it was rebuilt by Empress Maria Theresa in the latter half of the 18th century, giving it a formal Neo-Classical look. Today the castle is the official residence of the Czech president.

Prague Castle and the Vltava

1 Old Royal Palace
While Prince Bořivoj made do with a wooden structure, subsequent residences were built on top of each other as the tastes of Bohemia's rulers changed *(see p14)*. Halls are decorated with coats of arms **(above)**.

2 South Gardens
Emperor Ferdinand I and his son Maximilian II gave the castle some greenery in the late 16th century, and First Republic architect Josip Plečnik created the lined paths, steps and grottoes that extend to Malá Strana.

3 White Tower
The castle's White Tower was once used as a prison and torture chamber. Today, shops here sell grisly souvenirs. The gangways from which archers once watched over the moat are lined with replicas of weapons.

4 Lobkowicz Palace
The only privately owned building **(below)** in the castle complex, this rival to the National Gallery holds works by Bruegel, Canaletto, Dürer, Rubens and Velázquez in its collection.

5 St George's Convent
Prince Boleslav II, with Princess Mlada, established the first Czech convent for Benedictine nuns here in AD 973. The Romanesque building is not open to the public.

6 St George's Basilica
Prince Vratislav built the basilica around AD 920. The 13th-century chapel of St Ludmila, St Wenceslas's grandmother, is decorated with beautiful 16th-century paintings **(above)**.

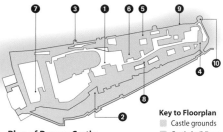

Plan of Prague Castle

Key to Floorplan
- Castle grounds
- Castle buildings

CASTLE GUIDE

Most of the grounds are free to enter, but tickets to see the interiors are sold at the information centres in the second and third courtyards. The shorter circuit takes in Golden Lane, the Old Royal Palace, St George's Basilica, St Vitus's and Daliborka Tower; the longer tour circuit adds the Powder Tower and the Rosenberg Palace. Tickets for other castle areas are also available.

8 Rosenberg Palace

This 16th-century palace has had multiple uses during its history: as an 18th-century residence for noblewomen, as part of the Ministry of Internal Affairs of Czechoslovakia and as modern presidential offices.

9 Golden Lane

In order to avoid paying guild dues in town, goldsmiths lived in these colourful little houses **(below)** that were built into the castle walls.

7 Chapel of the Holy Cross

Built by the Italian architect Anselmo Lurago in 1763, this chapel **(left)** houses the Treasure of St Vitus, which includes the sword of St Wenceslas.

10 Daliborka Tower

When captured, Dalibor, a Czech Robin Hood figure, became the first prisoner of the tower that now takes his name.

NEED TO KNOW

MAP C2 ▪ Hradčany ▪ 224 372423, 224 372434 ▪ Adm (various combination tickets available; check on the castle website) ▪ www.hrad.cz

Old Royal Palace, Golden Lane, St George's Basilica, Rosenberg Palace, Powder Tower, Daliborka Tower & Picture Gallery: Apr–Oct: 9am–5pm daily, Nov–Mar: 9am–4pm daily

Chapel of the Holy Cross, Great South Tower: 10am–6pm daily

Lobkowicz Palace: 10am–6pm Mon–Fri (from 9am Sat & Sun); www.lobkowicz.cz

Grounds: open 6am–10pm daily

▪ The guard at the gates changes on the hour and at noon there is a fanfare and flag ceremony in the first courtyard.

Old Royal Palace Features

Vaulted ceiling of the Vladislav Hall

1 Vladislav Hall

Here, Benedikt Rejt created a mastery of Gothic design with the elaborate vaulting. It has been used for coronations and jousting tournaments, and, since the First Republic, the country's presidents have been ceremoniously sworn in here.

2 Louis Wing

Only ten years and a few steps separate the southern wing from the main hall, but in that brief space, Rejt moved castle architecture from Gothic to Renaissance. Bohemian nobles met here in an administrative body when the king was away.

3 Bohemian Chancellery

Protestant noblemen threw two Catholic governors and their secretary from the east window, sparking off the Thirty Years' War. Their fall was broken by a dung heap – or an intervening angel, depending on who you ask.

4 Old Land Rolls Room

The coats of arms on the walls belong to clerks who tracked property ownership and court decisions from 1614 to 1777. Until Maria Theresa, records were unnumbered, identified only by elaborate covers.

5 Diet

Bohemian nobles met the king here in a prototype parliament. The king sat on the throne (the one seen today is a 19th-century replica), the archbishop sat on his right, while the estates sat on his left. The portraits on the wall show, from the left, Maria Theresa, her husband Franz, Josef II, Leopold II and Franz I, who fought Napoleon at Austerlitz.

6 Chapel of All Saints

A door leads from Vladislav Hall to a balcony above the Chapel of All Saints, modelled by Petr Parléř on Paris's Gothic Sainte-Chapelle. After fire destroyed it in 1541, it was redesigned in Renaissance style. Of particular artistic note is Hans van Aachen's *Triptych of the Angels*.

7 Soběslav Residence

Prince Soběslav built the first stone palace in the 12th century.

8 The Story of Prague Castle

This informative and entertaining exhibition covers the history, events, personalities and arts and crafts relating to the main castle complex.

9 Busts from Petr Parléř's Workshop

These impressive effigies, created in the late 14th century, include the grandfather-father-grandson set of John of Luxembourg, Charles IV and Wenceslas IV.

10 Riders' Staircase

The low steps and vaulted ceiling of this stairway permitted mounted knights to make grand entrances to the spectacular jousting tournaments held in Vladislav Hall.

The rib-vaulted Rider's Staircase

PRAGUE'S DEFENESTRATIONS

Prague's first recorded instance of execution by hurling the condemned people from a window occurred at the outset of the Hussite Wars in 1419. Vladislav II's officials met a similar fate in 1483. Perhaps as a tribute to their forebears, more than 100 Protestant nobles stormed the Old Royal Palace in 1618 and cast two hated Catholic governors and their secretary out of the window. Protestants said the men's fall was broken by a dung heap swept from the Vladislav Hall after a recent tournament, while Catholics claimed they were saved by angels. The incident is often cited as the spark that began the Thirty Years' War. After the defeat of the Protestants by the army of the Holy Roman Emperor Ferdinand II at the first skirmish at White Mountain *(see p42)*, 27 of these nobles were executed in the Old Town Square *(see pp18–21)*.

TOP 10
RULERS OF PRAGUE

1 Wenceslas (around 907–935)

2 Ottokar II (1233–78)

3 Charles IV (1316–78)

4 Wenceslas IV (1361–1419)

5 Rudolf II (1552–1612)

6 Tomáš Garrigue Masaryk (1850–1937)

7 Edvard Beneš (1884–1948)

8 Gustáv Husák (1913–1991)

9 Václav Havel (1936–2011)

10 Václav Klaus (b.1941)

The Battle of White Mountain (Bílá Hora) in 1620 played a role in the Counter-Reformation and the re-Catholization of the Czech lands.

The Defenestration of Prague, 23 May 1618 **(1889)** by Václav Brožík depicts the Protestants' attack on the Catholic governors. Painted 271 years after the event, it illustrates how the event remained in the Czech consciousness.

⭐ St Vitus Cathedral

The spectacular Gothic *Katedrála svatého Víta* is an unmissable sight in Prague, not least because of its dominant position on Hradčany hill, looming over the Vltava and the rest of the city. Prince Wenceslas first built a rotunda here on a pagan worship site and dedicated it to St Vitus *(svatý Vít)*, a Roman saint. Matthew d'Arras began work on the grand cathedral in 1344 when Prague was named an archbishopric. He died shortly thereafter and Charles IV hired the Swabian wunderkind Petr Parléř to take over. With the intervention of the Hussite Wars, however, work stopped and, remarkably, construction was only finally completed in 1929.

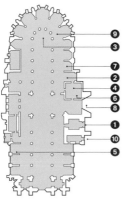

1 Great South Tower

The point at which the Hussite Wars halted construction of this 96-m (315-ft) tower is clear. When work resumed, architectural style had moved into the Renaissance, hence the rounded cap on a Gothic base **(left)**.

2 Royal Crypt

The greatest kings of Bohemia are buried in a single room beneath the cathedral, including Charles IV, Wenceslas IV and Rudolf II.

Plan of St Vitus Cathedral

3 High Altar

Bounded by St Vitus Chapel and the marble sarcophagi of Ferdinand I and family, the high altar and chancel follow a strict Neo-Gothic philosophy **(above)**.

Wenceslas Chapel 4

This stands on the site of the first rotunda and contains St Wenceslas's tomb. The frescoes of Christ's Passion on the lower wall are surrounded by 1,300 semi-precious stones. To celebrate his son Ludvik's coronation, Vladislav II commissioned the upper frescoes of St Wenceslas's life **(right)**.

5 New Archbishop's Chapel

Czech artists Alfons Mucha created the Art Nouveau window of the Slavic saints for the chapel **(left)**. Despite appearances, the glass is painted, not stained.

6 Bohemian Crown Jewels

You'd think there would be a safer place for the crown and sceptre of Bohemia, but the coronation chamber of Wenceslas Chapel is said to be guarded by the spirit of the saint.

PETR PARLÉŘ

After the death of Matthew d'Arras, Charles IV made the Swabian Petr Parléř his chief architect. Parléř undertook work on St Vitus Cathedral, Charles Bridge and numerous other Gothic monuments that still stand in Prague. He trained numerous artisans, and his talented sons and nephews continued his work after his death in 1399.

7 Royal Oratory

The royals crossed a narrow bridge from the Old Royal Palace *(see p12)* to this private gallery for Mass. The coats of arms represent all the countries ruled by Vladislav II.

8 Golden Portal

This triple-arched arcade **(above)** was the main entrance to the cathedral until the western end was completed in the 20th century.

9 The Tomb of St John of Nepomuk

The silver for this 1,680-kg (3,700-lb) coffin came from the Bohemian mining town Kutná Hora, signified by the miners' statues to the left of the tomb.

Sigismund 10

One of four Renaissance bells in the Great South Tower, the 18-tonne bell affectionately known as Sigismund is the nation's largest and dates from 1549. It takes four volunteers to ring the bell **(right)** on important church holidays and at events.

NEED TO KNOW

MAP C2 ■ Third Courtyard, Prague Castle ■ 224 372423/34 (castle info centres) ■ Adm (only combined tickets with the castle available; buy at the information centres in the castle courtyards) ■ www.katedralasvate hovita.cz

Cathedral: 9am–5pm Mon–Sat, noon–5pm Sun (to 4pm Nov–Mar)

Great South Tower: 10am–6pm daily (to 5pm Nov–Mar)

■ The entrance (western) areas of St Vitus Cathedral can be visited for free. Admission is charged for other areas.

■ The Royal Crypt may be entered with a guide.

TOP 10 ⭐ Old Town Square

As the heart and soul of the city, no visitor should, or is likely to miss the Old Town Square (Staroměstské náměstí). There was a marketplace here in the 11th century, but it was in 1338, when John of Luxembourg gave Prague's burghers permission to form a town council, that the Old Town Hall was built (see p20) and the square came into its own. Today, it has a lively atmosphere, with café tables set out in front of painted façades, hawkers selling their wares and horse-drawn carriages waiting to ferry tourists around.

1 Dům u Minuty
The "House at the Minutes" **(below)** probably takes its name from the not-so-minute *sgraffito* images on its walls. The alchemical symbols adorning Staroměstské náměstí 2 date from 1611. Writer Franz Kafka lived in the black-and-white house as a boy, from 1889 to 1896 (see p44).

Prague's beautiful Old Town Square

2 House at the Stone Bell
Formerly done up in Baroque style, workers discovered the Gothic façade of this house as late as 1980. On the southwestern corner is the bell which gives the house its name. The Municipal Gallery often hosts temporary exhibitions here.

3 Church of Our Lady before Týn
This Gothic edifice **(below)** began as a humble church serving residents in the mercantile town (týn) in the 14th century (see p49). Following architectural customs of the time, the south tower is stouter than the north one; they are said to depict Adam and Eve.

4 St Nicholas's Church
Prague has two Baroque churches of St Nicholas, both built by Kilian Ignac Dientzenhofer. The architect completed the one in Old Town **(above)** two years before starting Malá Strana's (see p94). Regular concerts here give visitors a chance to hear the church's organ (see p67).

Jan Hus Memorial

Hus was burned at the stake in 1415 for proposing radical church reform. The inscription below the figure of Hus **(right)** at the 1915 memorial reads "Truth Will Prevail".

JAN HUS

The rector of Prague (later Charles) University, Jan Hus was dedicated to fighting against corruption in the church. He was declared a heretic by the church, and was summoned to Germany where he was burned at the stake. Czech resentment turned into civil war, with Hussite rebels facing the power of Rome. But the Hussites split into moderate and radical factions, the former defeating the latter in 1434. Hus is still a national figure – 6 July, the day he was killed, is a public holiday.

7 Ungelt

The courtyard behind Týn church was home to foreign merchants in the 14th century, but today it houses smart boutiques and cafés.

8 Štorch House

At Staroměstské náměstí 16 **(left)**, the focal points are Art Nouveau paintings of St Wenceslas (the patron saint of Bohemia) and the three Magi (see p55).

6 Marian Column

On Czechoslovakia's declaration of independence in 1918, this former column reminded jubilant mobs of Habsburg rule and they tore it down. A plan is afoot to rebuild it.

9 Kinský Palace

This ornate Rococo palace now houses the National Gallery's collection of Asian art (see p46). It was once home to the haberdashery owned by Franz Kafka's father, Hermann.

NEED TO KNOW

MAP M3 ▪ Old Town

Old Town Hall: Staroměstské náměstí 1; 236 002629; Halls & Cellars: open 9am–6pm daily (from 11am Mon); Tower: open 9am–10pm daily (from 11am Mon); Adm (combined, family and reduced tickets available); www.staromestskaradnicepraha.cz

▪ Climbing on the Jan Hus Memorial or trampling the flowers could earn you a fine as well as embarrassment.

10 Malé náměstí

The ornate wrought-iron well in the centre of the "Small Square" doubles as a plague memorial. The elaborate murals of craftsmen on the façade of Rott House **(right)** were designed by Mikoláš Aleš. From the 19th century to the early 1990s, the building was an ironmongery.

Old Town Hall Features

Astronomical Clock

During the day, bells ring, cocks crow and 15th-century statues dance on the hour while crowds of tourists watch from below.

Apostles in the Astronomical Clock

2 Apostles

Marionette artist Vojtěch Sucharda carved the 12 wooden figures that emerge from the clock every hour – they replace the ones destroyed by German artillery in 1945.

3 Art Gallery

On the Old Town Hall's ground floor is an exhibition space which features temporary shows.

4 Dukla Memorial

Behind a brass plaque marked with the year 1944 is a pot of soil from the Dukla battlefield. German artillery gunned down 84,000 Red Army soldiers in this Slovak pass in one of the most grievous military miscalculations of World War II.

Dukla Memorial

5 White Mountain Memorial

In the pavement on the town hall's eastern side are set 27 crosses in memory of the Bohemian nobles who were executed for their role in the Thirty Years' War. After the Battle of White Mountain (see p42), the men were publicly hanged, beheaded or drawn and quartered here.

6 Gothic Chapel

The small chapel adjoining the Mayors' Hall was consecrated in 1381 in honour of Sts Wenceslas, Vitus and Ludmila. Wenceslas IV's emblem and his wife Eufemia's initial adorn the entrance portal. In the nave is a model of the Marian column which stood on the square until 1918 and may be rebuilt (see p19).

7 Elevator

The elevator to the viewing gallery of the tower won a design award in 1999. Oddly enough, its space-age design works harmoniously with the stony surroundings. It also permits wheelchair access to the top of the tower – a rare consideration in Prague.

8 Viewing Gallery

The parapet under the Old Town Hall's roof affords visitors a unique view of the square and the Old Town below. A little pocket change will buy you two minutes on a miniature telescope, with which you can admire the Prague Valley.

9 Gothic Cellars

The cellars of the Old Town Hall were once ground-floor rooms. The town was subject to flooding, so more earth was added to keep the burghers' feet dry. The spaces were used as granaries as well as debtors' prisons.

10 The Green

Retreating German artillery unloaded their guns on the Old Town Hall's north wing to avoid carrying the shells back to Berlin. After the war, the wing was torn down. Now the area is lined with stalls selling Czech handicrafts.

BUILDING THE OLD TOWN HALL

Prague's Old Town received its charter and fortifications from John of Luxembourg in 1338, but its town clerk had to wait nearly 150 years for an office. The Old Town Hall was cobbled together from existing houses over the centuries until it comprised the five houses that stand at Staroměstské náměstí 1–2 today. The town hall's eastern wing once stretched to within a few feet of St Nicholas's Church *(see p18)*, but in 1945 German artillery bombardment reduced it to rubble. The 69.5-m (228-ft) tower was built in 1364, and in 1410 the imperial clockmaker Mikuláš of Kadaň created the basic mechanism of the Prague Orloj, or Astronomical Clock. In 1552 Jan Táborský was put in charge, and by 1566 the clock was fully mechanized.

**TOP 10
FEATURES OF THE
ASTRONOMICAL
CLOCK**

1 Solar clock
2 Lunar clock
3 Josef Mánes Calendar
4 Apostles
5 Angel and the Sciences
6 Vanity, Avarice, Death and Lust
7 Rooster
8 Hourly shows
9 Mikuláš of Kadaň
10 Dial

The Astronomical Clock not only tells the time, but also displays the movement of the sun and moon through the signs of the zodiac, and of the planets around the earth. The calendar plate below the clock has paintings by 19th-century Czech artist Josef Mánes.

★ Charles Bridge

The spectacular Charles Bridge *(Karlův most)* has witnessed processions, battles, executions and, increasingly, film shoots since its construction between 1357 and 1402. Architect Petr Parléř built it in Gothic style to replace its predecessor, the Judith Bridge. The bridge's most distinguishing feature is its gallery of 30 statues. The religious figures were installed from 1683 onwards to lead people back to the church. Some, such as Bohn's Calvary, are politically controversial; others, such as Braun's St Luitgard, are incomparably lovely. Today all the statues are copies, with the originals preserved in museums across the city.

Old Town Bridge Tower

From the parapet of the Old Town bridge tower, you can see the gentle S-curve that Petr Parléř *(see p17)* built into the bridge to obstruct invaders, as well as a jaw-dropping panorama of the city.

2 Calvary

This statue will cause double takes among students of Hebrew. According to a nearby apologia, the words "Holy, holy, holy is the Lord of Hosts" were added in 1696, paid for by a local Jewish man who had been accused of profaning the cross.

Charles Bridge and the Old Town bridge tower

3 The Lorraine Cross

Midway across the bridge is a brass cross **(below)** where John of Nepomuk's body was thrown into the river *(see p43)*. It is said that wishes made at the cross will come true.

4 Statue of St John of Nepomuk

At the base of the statue of St John **(right)** is a brass relief showing a man diving into the river. Rubbing it to attract good luck is an old local tradition; petting the adjacent brass dog is a new one.

5 Statue of Sts Cyril and Methodius

Greek missionaries who brought both Christianity and the Cyrillic alphabet to the Czech and Slovak lands, Cyril and Methodius are revered figures in both countries to this day. Karel Dvořák created this statue in 1928–1938 at the peak of Czechoslovakia's National Awakening following independence.

6 Statue of Bruncvik

Peer over the bridge's southern edge to see the Czech answer to King Arthur. Bruncvik (left), a mythical Bohemian knight, is said to have had a magical sword and helped a lion fight a seven-headed dragon. He and his army are promised to awaken and save Prague at the city's most desperate hour.

7 Our Lady of the Mangles

The portrait of Mary hanging on the house south of the bridge is tied to an ancient tale of miraculous healing. Seeing the light go out on the balcony below is supposedly an omen of imminent death – don't stare too long.

8 Statue of St Luitgard

Matthias Braun's 1710 depiction of a blind Cistercian nun's celebrated vision, in which Christ appeared to her and permitted her to touch his wounds, has a timeless appeal (right).

NEED TO KNOW

MAP J4 ■ en.muzeum prahy.cz/prague-towers

Malá Strana bridge tower: 607 050434

Old Town bridge tower: 224 220569

Open Apr–Sep: 10am–10pm; Nov–Feb: 10am–6pm; Mar & Oct: 10am–8pm (both towers)

Adm (both towers)

■ The Malá Strana bridge tower houses an exhibit on the bridge's history. The Old Town bridge tower has an exhibit on Charles IV and the bridge.

9 Antonín

One of many artists on the bridge, the popular Antonín mostly painted portraits of himself as the devil. His proximity to the Čertovka (Devil's Canal) may have been the key to his choice of subject.

10 Statue of the Trinitarian Order

This religious order was set up to ransom prisoners of war from the Crusades and buy Christians back their freedom, hence the depiction of a bored Turk keeping guard outside a cell (left).

WHEN TO VISIT CHARLES BRIDGE

During summer, and increasingly year-round, the bridge is well nigh impassable throughout the day, crowded with artists, tourists and the odd Dixieland jazz band. It is best seen in the early hours as the sun rises over the Old Town bridge tower. A late evening stroll gives a similarly dramatic view, with the illuminated cathedral and castle looming above.

🔟 ⭐ The Loreto

At the heart of this sparkling 17th-century Baroque pilgrimage site is its claim to fame and most proud possession: a replica of the original Santa Casa in Loreto, Italy, believed to be the house where the Virgin Mary received the Incarnation. Construction of the grandiose church and the surrounding chapels coincided with the Counter-Reformation, and one of Prague's first Baroque buildings was intended to lure Czechs back to the Catholic faith.

1 Loretánské náměstí

This square is said to have been a pagan burial ground. The stucco façade of The Loreto (right) is dwarfed by the Černín Palace opposite, home of the Ministry of Foreign Affairs.

Plan of The Loreto

2 Santa Casa

The stucco reliefs on the outside of this replica (above) of the Holy Family's house in Nazareth depict scenes from the life of the Virgin Mary. Inside stands the miracle-working statue of Our Lady of Loreto.

3 Bell Tower

The carillon was the gift of a merchant of Prague whose daughter was healed by the intercession of the Lady of Loreto. An automated mechanism chimes a Marian hymn every hour.

4 Inner Courtyard

In this courtyard, visitors can admire two Baroque fountains (right). The south fountain depicts the Assumption of the Virgin; the north features a sculpture of the Resurrection.

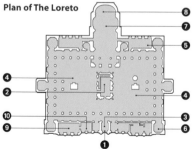

Previous pages Sunset over Charles Bridge, with Prague Castle in the background

5 Arcade

Before and after visiting the Santa Casa, pilgrims passed through the arcade and prayed at its chapels dedicated to the Holy Family, the Holy Rood, St Francis Seraphim, St Antony of Padua, St Anne and Our Lady of Sorrows.

6 St Wilgefortis Altar

The Chapel of Our Lady of Sorrows contains the altar of a bearded, crucified woman. Wilgefortis (Starosta in Czech) was said to be a Portuguese maiden who prayed for a masculine appearance in order to preserve her chastity.

SANTA CASA

The Santa Casa was the house in Nazareth in which the archangel Gabriel is believed to have announced to the Virgin Mary that she would conceive the Son of God. In the 13th century, the Greek Angeli family moved the house to Loreto, Italy. As the Marian cult spread, copies of the Italian Loreto started emerging all over Europe – the 17th-century Prague site is believed to be the truest representation of the original structure.

8 Altars of Sts Felicissimus and Marcia

On either side of the altar in the Church of the Nativity are large reliquary displays containing the remains of these two Spanish saints.

9 Treasury

The Communists created this exhibit of sacred gold and silver items **(right)** to show how the church brought peasants to obedience with a "cheap promise of happiness beyond the grave".

7 Church of the Nativity

Originally a small alcove behind the Santa Casa, the church **(left)** was expanded into its present size in 1717. The Rococo organ stands opposite the altar, over a crypt to Loreto benefactors.

NEED TO KNOW

MAP B2 ▪ Loretánské náměstí 7 ▪ 220 516740 ▪ www.loreta.cz

Open Apr–Oct: 9am–5pm daily; Nov–Mar: 9:30am–4pm daily

Adm (under-6s free, family tickets available); audio guides can be hired

▪ At Kapucínská 2 nearby is a memorial to people tortured by secret police in the former Interior Ministry building.

10 Prague Sun

The silver monstrance **(left)** for displaying the host – created in 1699 by Johann Bernard Fischer von Erlach – is gold-plated and studded with 6,222 diamonds. The Virgin looks up at her son, represented by the host in the receptacle.

🔟 ⭐ Old Jewish Cemetery

The crumbling Old Jewish Cemetery *(Starý židovský hřbitov)* is a moving memorial to the once considerable Jewish community of Prague. This was one of the few burial sites available to the city's Jews, and graves had to be layered when the plot became full. Estimates put it at about 100,000 graves, with the oldest headstone dating from 1439 and the final burial taking place in 1787. The Old-New Synagogue, built in the 13th century, is situated across the street.

1 Avigdor Kara's Grave
The oldest grave is that of this poet and scholar, best known for his documentation of the pogrom of 1389, which he survived.

2 Mordechai Maisel's Grave
Mordechai Maisel (1528–1601), the mayor of the Jewish ghetto during the reign of Rudolf II, funded the synagogue that bears his name *(see p110)*.

3 Grave of Rabbi Judah Loew
The grave of Rabbi Judah Loew ben Bezalel *(see p110)*, to whom legend attributes the creation of the Prague Golem *(see p60)*, is located here **(left)**.

Gravestones, Old Jewish Cemetery

4 Gothic Tombstones
The eastern wall has fragments of Gothic tombstones rescued from another graveyard near Vladislavova street in 1866. Further graves at another site were found in the 1990s.

GRAVE SYMBOLS

A Hebrew tombstone *(matzevah)* as a rule contains the deceased's name, date of death and eulogy. In addition, the grave markers here often included symbolic images indicating the lineage of the deceased. Names are often symbolized by animals, according to biblical precedent or Hebrew or Germanic translations – David Gans's tombstone features a goose *(gans* in German). Some professions are also represented: scissors may appear on a tailor's tombstone, for example.

5 Klausen Synagogue
Mordechai Maisel also commissioned the building of the Klausen Synagogue *(see p110)* on the cemetery's northern edge **(above)**. It now houses exhibitions on Jewish festivals and traditions *(see p47)*.

6 Nephele Mound
Stillborn children, miscarried babies and other infants who died under a year old were buried in the southeast corner of the cemetery.

7 David Gans's Tombstone

Gans's headstone **(left)** is marked with a goose and the Star of David, after his name and his faith. A pupil of Loew, Gans (1541–1613) was the author of a seminal two-volume history of the Jewish people. He was also an accomplished astronomer during the time of Johannes Kepler *(see p43)*.

8 Grave of Rabbi Oppenheim

Rabbi David Oppenheim was the first chief rabbi of Moravia, and later chief rabbi of Bohemia and finally of Prague, where he died in 1736.

9 Zemach Grave

The gravestone of the printer Mordechai Zemach (d. 1592) and his son Bezalel (d. 1589) lies next to the Pinkas Synagogue *(see p111)*. Mordechai Zemach was a co-founder of the Prague Burial Society.

NEED TO KNOW

MAP K2 ■ Josefov

Old Jewish Cemetery:
U Starého hřbitova 3; 222 317191; open Apr–Oct: 9am–6pm Sun–Fri (to 4:30pm Nov–Mar); closed Jewish holidays; Adm (ticket valid for 1 week, includes entrance to various synagogues; audio guides available; www.jewishmuseum.cz

Old-New Synagogue:
Červená; open 9am–6pm Sun–Fri (to 5pm Nov–Mar); Adm (under-6s free); www.synagogue.cz

■ In the synagogues, it is customary for men to wear a *yarmulka* (skull cap). Look for them at the entrance; return them when you leave.

■ The Museum of Decorative Arts' east windows *(see p47)* offer excellent crowd-free views of the cemetery.

10 Hendl Bassevi's Grave

This elaborate tombstone **(below)** marks the resting place of the "Jewish Queen", Hendl Bassevi. Her husband, mayor Jacob Bassevi, was raised to the nobility by Ferdinand II and permitted a coat of arms, which can be seen on his wife's gravestone.

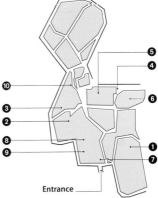

Entrance

Plan of the Old Jewish Cemetery

Old-New Synagogue Features

1 **Rabbi Loew's Chair**
Topped with a Star of David, the tall chair found by the eastern wall has been reserved for the chief rabbis of Prague throughout the history of the synagogue.

2 **Jewish Standard**
Prague's Jewish community was permitted a banner in the 15th century as a symbol of its autonomy. The copy hanging above the bimah replicates a 1716 original, featuring a Jewish hat within a six-pointed star and bearing the legend "Shema Yisroel".

The nave of the synagogue

3 **Nave**
Twelve narrow windows, evoking the 12 tribes of Israel, line the perimeter walls, which are unadorned save for the abbreviation of biblical verses. Two central pillars are modelled on the façade columns of the Temple of Jerusalem.

4 **Ark**
Behind the curtain on the eastern wall are the Torah scrolls, which are kept in the holy ark. The tympanum features foliage and grape motifs, which are also found in the nearby Convent of St Agnes (see pp34–5), and date from the synagogue's construction in the late 13th century.

5 **Entrance**
The biblical inscription "Revere God and observe His commandments! For this applies to all mankind" admonished worshippers as they were entering and leaving the synagogue.

6 **Vaulting**
To avoid forming the sign of the cross, a fifth rib was added to the nave's vaulting, which is decorated with vine leaves and ivy.

7 **Women's Windows**
Women were not permitted in the nave of the synagogue, but sat in the vestibule. Narrow openings in the wall allowed them to follow the services being conducted within.

8 **Bimah**
A pulpit stands on this dais in the centre. From here the rabbi reads the Torah and performs wedding ceremonies.

9 **Josefov Town Hall**
Adjacent to the synagogue stands the Jewish Town Hall. The hands of the clock on the façade run anticlockwise – or clockwise if you read Hebrew (see p110).

10 **Attic**
Legend has it that Rabbi Judah Loew stashed the remains of the Golem he had created (see p60) under the synagogue's large saddle roof.

The roof and attic of the synagogue

THE JEWS IN PRAGUE

Prague's Jews have suffered anti-Semitic behaviour almost since their arrival in the 10th century. Zealous Christians destroyed an early settlement in what is now Malá Strana. Such pogroms were not uncommon – the most infamous is the Passover slaughter of 1389, in which rioters killed more than 3,000 Jews, including those who had taken refuge in the Old-New Synagogue. But there were also high points. Prominent Jews, notably Rabbi Loew *(see p110)* and Mordechai Meisel, enjoyed influence in the court of Rudolf II; Charles VI recognized the community's autonomy in 1716; his descendant Joseph II ended many discriminatory measures; and in the late 19th century Jews were active in the National Revival. However, anti-Semitism still lurked. In 1899, Leopold Hilsner was accused of ritual murder; his legal counsel was Tomáš Garrigue Masaryk, future president of independent Czechoslovakia. Although the interwar years were a golden age for Czech Jews, among them Franz Kafka *(see p44)*, the 1938 Munich Agreement paved the way for Hitler to take possession of Czech lands, and the Jews were restricted to a ghetto before being deported to Nazi concentration camps. Synagogues were turned into archives for looted Jewish artifacts. Hitler reportedly even planned to create a museum of the Jews as an extinct race in Josefov. By the end of the war nearly 80,000 Jews from Bohemia and Moravia had died in the Holocaust.

Terezín was a holding camp north of Prague to which the capital's Jews were moved by the Nazis during World War II. From there, many were later transported to Nazi-run extermination camps in occupied Poland.

**TOP 10
JEWISH LEADERS**

1 Eliezer ben Elijah Ashkenazi (1512–85)

2 Judah Loew ben Bezalel (c. 1520–1609)

3 Mordechai Meisel (1528–1601)

4 Mordechai ben Abraham Jaffe (1530–1612)

5 Ephraim Solomon ben Aaron of Luntshits (1550–1619)

6 Joseph Solomon Delmedigo (1591–1655)

7 David ben Abraham Oppenheim (1664–1736)

8 Yechezkel ben Yehuda Landau (1713–93)

9 Solomon Judah Lieb Rapoport (1790–1867)

10 Efraim Karol Sidon (b. 1942)

TOP 10 ⭐ Trade Fair Palace

Surrounded by the Art Nouveau tenement buildings of Holešovice, the austere Trade Fair Palace *(Veletržní Palác)* is a daring work of art in itself. It was the first official Functionalist building in Europe, and even Le Corbusier was impressed when he visited Prague in 1928. In 1979, plans were launched to turn the former trade fair complex into the home of the National Gallery's modern and contemporary art collection. The space was inaugurated in 1995, with works by prominent Czech artists alongside a rich array of international masters from the 19th, 20th and 21st centuries.

1 House in Aix-en-Provence

The National Gallery's impressive collection of French art was begun in 1923, when Czech president Tomáš Masaryk helped found a small collection. This bright work showing a large tan house (c. 1887) by Paul Cézanne was one of those original 25 pieces.

4 Green Wheat

Van Gogh's encounter with Impressionism was a decisive moment. Charmed by the southern French countryside, he created bright canvases such as this 1889 landscape **(above)**.

2 Bonjour, Monsieur Gauguin

Paul Gauguin originally painted this simple, flat self-portrait **(above)** as a decoration for the lower panel of a dining-room door in an inn in Le Pouldu, Brittany. The much-admired 19th-century French artist painted this enlarged copy in 1889.

5 St John the Baptist

Auguste Rodin's 1878 sculpture is a study of spiral motion, from the tension of the firmly anchored feet, to the rotating trunk, to the head turned away from the dominant gesture of the right hand **(left)**.

3 Anxiety

Otto Gutfreund paved the way for modern Czech sculpture. This bronze 1912 work captures the apprehension of man in the early 20th century.

6 Jaguar Attacking a Horseman

Delacroix often visited zoos to study predatory animals whose movement inspired him. This 1855 canvas, striking for its interaction of colour and motion, is an example of his research.

7 Head of a Young Girl

Henri Laurens's 1926 bronze sculpture is a synthesis of Cubism and the classical ideal of form and beauty. It was added to the collections in 1935.

NEED TO KNOW

MAP B5 ■ Dukelských hrdinů 47, Holešovice ■ 224 301122
■ www.ngprague.cz

Open 10am–6pm Tue–Sun

Adm

■ The café on the ground floor offers a welcome respite.

■ The first floor houses temporary exhibits; check the gallery's website for details. The exhibits shown on these pages are all located on the third floor.

8 At the Moulin Rouge

Toulouse-Lautrec thrived on depictions of Paris nightlife such as this oil tempera on cardboard. One of the dancing women is his muse, Jane Avril. Oscar Wilde is one of the figures in the background.

9 Myself, Self Portrait

With the city of Paris and the elements of modern civilization in the background, Henri Rousseau's self-portrait, painted in 1890, depicts the artist as a self-assured personality **(right)**.

10 Self-Portrait

One of 14 Picassos donated in 1960 by former National Museum director Vincenc Kramář, the almond-shaped eyes and triangular nose of this 1907 work testify to the influence of Iberian art.

GALLERY HISTORY

Plans for a trade fair complex began in 1924. A design competition selected the work of architects Oldřich Týl and Josef Fuchs. Only the existing Trade Fair Palace was completed; the other planned buildings never materialized due to a lack of funding. The Trade Fair Palace opened in 1928 on the 10th anniversary of the Republic. It was badly damaged by fire in 1974 and was reopened to the public as a gallery in 1995.

Plan of the third floor of Trade Fair Palace

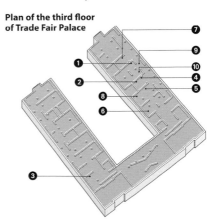

🔟⭐ Convent of St Agnes

The 13th-century Convent of St Agnes of Bohemia *(Klášter sv. Anežky)* is an impressive Gothic building closely tied to Czech statehood. Daughter of Czech King Přemyšl Ottokar I, Princess Agnes chose a spiritual life and founded a convent here in 1234 for the Poor Clares, an order of nuns associated with the Order of St Francis. However, it was Agnes's diplomatic skills and work in establishing the convent which raised Bohemia in the eyes of Rome, as much as any courtly efforts to do the same. Restored in the 1980s to its original splendour, the convent is now part of the National Gallery and exhibits its collection of medieval and early Renaissance art.

1 Strakonice Madonna
This larger-than-life, 700-year-old statue of the Virgin and Child is the Czech National Gallery's most prized possession. The gestures of the Madonna are strikingly rigid, and evoke the Classical French sculpture found in places such as Reims Cathedral.

2 Zbraslav Madonna
Bohemia's most celebrated Marian painting is evocative of Byzantine icons in its style. The ring on the Madonna's left-hand finger symbolizes the church through the mystical marriage between Christ and the Virgin Mary. The work was moved to the Convent of St Agnes from the Cistercian Zbraslav Monastery where the majority of the Přemyslid kings were laid to rest.

3 Vyšší Brod Altarpiece
The 14th-century cycle begins with the *Annunciation*, then proceeds through the *Adoration of the Magi* to *Pentecost* **(right)**. The creator of these beautiful panels is unknown.

4 Works of Master Theodoricus

Parts of an altar set on loan from Karlštejn Castle, these works include *St Charlemagne*, *St Catherine*, *St Matthew* **(left)**, *St Luke*, *St Ambrose* and *St Gregory*.

ST AGNES OF BOHEMIA

St Agnes of Bohemia was a powerful figure in medieval politics. Gregory IX granted special privileges to her convent and his successor Innocent IV sent priceless relics to be housed there. Agnes died in 1282, but her influence on Czech statehood was felt centuries later when, in 1989, Pope John Paul II canonized her; five days later, the Velvet Revolution began *(see p43)*.

5 Třeboň Altarpiece

Only three of the five double-sided panels of the 14th-century retable Třebon Altarpiece **(left)** have survived to the present day.

6 Capuchin Cycle

The origin of these 14 panels is unknown. The Virgin Mary is flanked by St Peter on the left and Christ on the right.

Plan of the Convent of St Agnes

Velhartice Altarpiece 7

Originating in south Bohemia around 1500, this is a rare example of a completely preserved altar **(right)**. Beneath the Madonna, cherubs hold the *vera* icon.

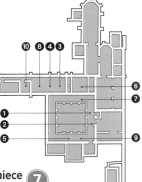

8 Martyrdom of St Florian

Albrecht Altdorfer created this painting **(below)** as part of a multipanel altar featuring scenes from the legend of St Florian. Other pieces from the series are in Florence.

NEED TO KNOW

MAP M1
- U Milosrdných 17
- 224 810628
- www.ngprague.cz

Open 10am–6pm Tue–Sun

Adm

- With the exception of short-term exhibitions, the ground floor of the convent building is empty, but the chamber music concerts that are frequently performed here give visitors the chance to appreciate the pure Gothic spaces.

9 Puchner Altarpiece

St Agnes gave up a life at court to pursue a spiritual vocation. On this 15th-century altarpiece, she is typically depicted nursing the sick.

10 Apocalypse Cycle

Although Albrecht Dürer is considered the foremost German Renaissance artist, he is best known to many for his woodcuts, such as this series of 15 **(left)**, which date from 1498 and retain a strong Gothic flavour.

TOP 10 ⭐ Wenceslas Square

This former medieval horse market began to be redeveloped in the 19th century, rapidly becoming the commercial hub of Prague. In 1848 it was renamed Wenceslas Square *(Václavské náměstí)* in honour of Bohemia's patron saint. The majority of the buildings seen today date from the early 20th century, and their beautiful Art Nouveau façades illustrate how keenly this style was embraced by Czech architects of the time. The square has often been the scene of historic events, most recently in 1989, when large, jubilant crowds gathered here to celebrate the end of Communism.

1 National Museum

Invading Warsaw Pact troops shelled the Neo-Renaissance building in 1968, mistaking it for the country's parliament (you can still see the pock-marks). The small entry fee is worth it, if only to see the grand marble stairway **(left)** and pantheon of Czech cultural figures *(see p118)*.

Wenceslas Square

St Wenceslas Statue 2

The Přemyslid prince sits astride a horse flanked by other Czech patrons **(right)** in Josef Myslbek's 1912 sculpture. The area "under the tail" is a traditional meeting place for locals.

3 Communist Memorial

In front of St Wenceslas is a memorial to the victims of Communism, such as the two men who died protesting against the 1968 invasion.

4 Palác Lucerna

Václav Havel's grandfather designed and built this building, now home to an art gallery, cinema, cafés, shops and a ballroom.

Palác Koruna 5

Built in 1912 in Geometric Modernist style, this "palace" **(right)** held offices, homes and Turkish-style baths. The listed building now hosts the Koruna Palace shopping centre, which boasts several cafés and luxury stores.

HISTORIC DEMONSTRATIONS

Wenceslas Square saw its first demonstration in 1419 when Catholic reformer Jan Želivský led a procession to St Stephen's Church. On 28 October 1918 the area witnessed Czechoslovak independence. In 1969, student Jan Palach set himself on fire here as a political protest against the Soviet occupation. It is still the scene of political protests today.

Grand Hotel Evropa

It's gone to seed over the years, but the Art Nouveau building **(right)** preserves its original façade and decor. Although it is closed for renovation until 2018, its architectural features can still be seen.

7 Upside-Down Statue

Hanging in the central passage of the Palác Lucerna is David Černý's take on Czech patron saint Wenceslas *(see p58)*.

8 Franciscan Garden

A stone's throw from the busy Wenceslas Square, this former monastery garden **(below)** provides much-needed peace from the city bustle *(see p115)*.

9 Svobodné slovo Balcony

During the Velvet Revolution *(see p43)*, Václav Havel addressed supporters from the balcony of the *Svobodné slovo* newspaper building. When the deposed Alexander Dubček joined him, the crowds knew that Communism was over.

10 Church of Our Lady of the Snows

Founded by Charles IV upon his coronation in 1347, this beautiful church **(above)** was to have been more than 100 m (330 ft) long, but it was never completed.

NEED TO KNOW

MAP N6 ■ New Town

■ Cafés line both sides of the lively square from top to bottom.

■ Owing to the high volume of tourists, Wenceslas Square is where pickpockets are most active. Be especially wary at the square's north end.

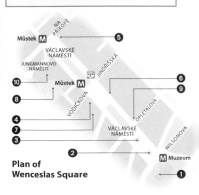

Plan of Wenceslas Square

TOP 10 ⭐ Petřín Hill

Covered with forests and orchards and dotted with strolling lovers, Petřín Hill is a soft counterpoint to the spires of Hradčany on the Vltava's left bank. Rising more than 300 m (1,000 ft) above sea level, the area began life as a vineyard in the 15th century, but has been a public park since 1825. Early chronicles say it was the site of pagan rituals to the god Perun, and believers still practise ancient rites here on 1 May each year. Above all, however, it is the perfect escape from the bustling city crowds.

Observation Tower **1**

Modelled after the Eiffel Tower in Paris, Petřín Hill's 63.5-m (210-ft) *Eiffelovka* stands only one-quarter as high as its inspiration. The tower was created for the Jubilee Exposition of 1891. A climb of 299 stairs leads to the viewing platform **(right)**.

2 Strahov Stadium

It may be ugly, but Strahov Stadium **(below)** is the largest arena of its kind in the world. It was built for Sokol, a physical exercise organization, and used for gymnastic rallies. Today it is a rock concert venue *(see p50)*.

NEED TO KNOW

MAP B4 ▪ Malá Strana

Funicular: open 9am–11:30pm daily; adm; www.dpp.cz

Observation Tower & Mirror Maze: open Apr–Sep: 10am–10pm; Mar & Oct: 10am–8pm; Nov–Feb: 10am–6pm, adm; en.muzeumprahy.cz/prague-towers

Strahov Monastery: open 9am–noon, 1–5pm daily; adm; www.strahovsky

klaster.cz

Church of St Michael, Church of St Lawrence: Closed to the public except during Masses (Sun, Mon or Fri)

Štefánik's Observatory: opening hours vary throughout the year; adm

▪ Nebozízek restaurant (Petřínské sady 411) offers spectacular views.

▪ There is also a café in the entrance hall of the Observation Tower.

3 Strahov Monastery

Founded in 1140, Strahov houses the nation's oldest books in the Strahov Library **(below)** while still functioning as a monastery. The Theological Hall, with its frescoes and statue of St John, is a must-see.

6 Karel Hynek Mácha Statue

Mácha is a national poet, best loved for his Romantic poem "May". On 1 May, admirers lay flowers at his statue.

4 Hunger Wall

The 14th-century wall **(above)** was once part of the city's southern fortifications. Charles IV is said to have ordered its construction as a project to feed the poor during a famine.

7 Church of St Michael

Still used for services, this lovely little 17th-century wooden church **(below)** was moved to Prague when the Ukraine valley it stood in was flooded by a dammed up river.

8 Štefánik's Observatory

Operating since 1928, the observatory **(below)** was named after M R Štefánik, a Slovak diplomat and co-founder of the Czechoslovak Republic, as well as a scientist and astronomer.

5 Mirror Maze

After laughing at the distorting mirrors in the labyrinth *(see p64)*, take in a bit of history with a diorama depicting the final battle of the Thirty Years' War on Charles Bridge.

9 Church of St Lawrence

Facing the mirror maze is this onion-domed church, built on a pagan shrine in the 10th century and rebuilt in Baroque style in the 18th century.

STRAHOV MONASTERY EXHIBITS

Strahov has suffered pillaging armies, fires and totalitarian regimes. Josef II dissolved most local monasteries in 1783, sparing Strahov on the condition that the monks conduct research at their library. Today the majority of the research involves paper preservation. On display are old books, pictures, ornate gospels and miniature Bibles.

10 Funicular

If you want to save your breath, do as visitors have done since 1890 and take the funicular railway to the top of the hill and walk down. The cable car offers outstanding views of the castle to the north.

The Top 10 of Everything

Moments in History	42
Writers and Composers	44
Museums and Galleries	46

The Smetana Embankment and the Novotný Bank seen from the Vltava

Places of Worship	**48**
Communist Monuments	**50**
Parks and Gardens	**52**
House Signs	**54**
Off the Beaten Track	**58**
Haunted Places	**60**
Eccentric Prague	**62**
Children's Attractions	**64**

Performing Arts Venues	**66**
Clubs	**68**
Restaurants	**70**
Prague Dishes	**72**
Bars and Kavárnas	**74**
Shops and Markets	**76**
Prague for Free	**78**
Festivals	**80**

🔟 Moments in History

Icon of Wenceslas in a Prague church

1 Wenceslas Assassinated

The "Good King" (actually a duke) was the second Christian ruler of Czech lands, succeeding his grandfather Bořivoj. Wenceslas I solidified ties with Rome and with German merchants. Murdered by his brother Boleslav the Cruel in 935, he was later canonized.

2 Charles IV Becomes Holy Roman Emperor

Grandson of an emperor and son of a Přemyslid princess, Charles could hardly help rising to the Bohemian throne in 1347 and to the Roman one in 1355. Prague became the seat of imperial power under his reign, as well as an archbishopric and the home of Central Europe's first university.

Statue of Charles IV in Křižovnické náměstí

3 Hussite Wars

After the Church Council at Constance burned Catholic reformer Jan Hus at the stake in 1415 *(see p19)*, his followers literally beat their ploughshares into swords and rebelled against both church and crown. The animosity that resulted between Protestant Czechs and German Catholics would continue to rage for centuries.

4 Reign of Rudolf II

The melancholy Rudolf II (1552–1611), who became Holy Roman Emperor in 1576, was not much good as a statesman and was under threat from his ambitious brother, Matthias, but he was a liberal benefactor

Rudolf II

of the arts and sciences. Among Rudolf's achievements were the support of Johannes Kepler's studies of planetary motion. The emperor also promoted religious freedom.

5 Battle of White Mountain

The Protestant nobility and the emperor continued to provoke each other until hostilities broke into open war. Imperial forces devastated the Czechs in the first battle of the Thirty Years' War in 1620 *(see p15)*. Czech lands were re-Catholicized, but resentment against Vienna and Rome continued to smoulder.

6 Independence

While World War I raged, National Revival leaders such as Tomáš Masaryk turned to the United States for support for an independent Czechoslovakia. As the war drew to a close in 1918, the Czechoslovak Republic was born.

7 World War II

The First Republic had barely stretched its legs when the Munich Agreement of 1938 gave Czech lands to Nazi Germany. Nearly 80,000 Czech Jews and Romany died in the Holocaust (see p31). After the war, the nation exacted revenge by expelling its German citizens.

Hitler in Prague's Hradčany, 1939

8 Rise of Communism

Grateful to the Russian Red Army for liberating the city of Prague in 1945, Czechoslovakia gave Soviet Communism the benefit of the doubt in the February 1948 elections.

9 Prague Spring

In 1968 First Secretary of the Communist Party Alexander Dubček introduced economic and social reforms that did not sit well with Moscow. Warsaw Pact troops and tanks swept through the streets of Prague, killing scores of protestors.

Tanks in the streets, Prague Spring

10 Velvet Revolution

After 10 days of mass protests in 1989, the Communist government bowed to the population's indignation. Czechs proudly recall that not even a single window was broken during the revolt.

TOP 10 HISTORICAL FIGURES

Johannes Kepler and Tycho Brahe

1 St Agnes (1211–82)
St Agnes, devout sister of Wenceslas I, built a convent for the order of the Poor Clares (the female counterpart of the Franciscans).

2 St John of Nepomuk (1340–93)
Wenceslas IV killed Nepomuk over the election of an abbot and threw his body from Charles Bridge.

3 Jan Hus (1370–1415)
Philosopher priest Jan Hus preached against church corruption and was burned as a heretic.

4 Mordechai Maisel (1528–1601)
The Jewish mayor was one of the richest men in Europe (see p28).

5 Tycho Brahe (1546–1601)
Astronomer at Rudolf's court, Brahe suffered a burst bladder when he refused to leave the emperor's side at a banquet.

6 Edward Kelley (1555–97) and John Dee (1527–c. 1608)
The English charlatans gained the trust of Rudolf II by converting lead into gold, but were said to be more interested in necromancy.

7 Johannes Kepler (1571–1630)
The German astronomer pioneered studies of planetary motion.

8 Albrecht von Wallenstein (1583–1634)
Leader of the Catholics during the Thirty Years' War, General Wallenstein built a vast palace in Prague (see p96).

9 Franz Kafka (1883–1924)
Prague's best-known author, Kafka was largely unpublished in his lifetime (see p44).

10 Emil Zátopek (1922–2000)
"The Locomotive" won three gold medals for long-distance events at the 1952 Olympic Games.

🔟 Writers and Composers

Franz Kafka was born in Prague

1 Franz Kafka

Although he wrote in German and almost none of his work was published in his lifetime, Franz Kafka *is* Prague. Many of his disturbing novels seem to foresee the Communist years. His peripatetic wanderings across this city, brooding features and death by tuberculosis all add to the mystique.

2 Gustav Meyrink

Almost completely unknown outside Austria and Germany, Gustav Meyrink is nevertheless responsible for one of Prague's most marketable notions: the Golem. In 1915 he wrote a novel drawing upon the legend of the clay automaton *(see p60)*, created then deactivated and locked in the Old-New Synagogue's attic by the Prague rabbi Judah Loew *(see p110)*.

3 Karel Čapek

This Czech writer is best known for his science fiction and

psychologically penetrating novels. With his 1920 play *R.U.R. (Rossum's Universal Robots)* he gave the world a word for an automaton, from the Czech word *robota*, meaning "forced labour".

Karel Čapek

4 Jaroslav Hašek

A notorious joker and the author of the celebrated satirical dig at the Austrian army, *The Good Soldier Švejk* (published in 1921), Hašek was also the creator of the Party for Moderate Progress Within the Bounds of the Law.

5 Wolfgang Amadeus Mozart

Prague and Vienna continue to duel over the legacy of the musical genius, with the Czechs always claiming that Mozart loved them better. The composer premiered his opera *Don Giovanni* in Prague's Estates Theatre *(see p67)* and Prague residents mourned his death in 1791. Regular Mozart concerts are held in the city.

Mozart

6 Bedřich Smetana

The composer wrote his opera *Libuše*, based on the legendary princess, for the reopening of Prague's National Theatre in 1883. Smetana vies with Antonín Dvořák for the title of best-loved Czech composer; the former's ode to beer in *The Bartered Bride* gives him a certain advantage.

7 Antonín Dvořák

The works of Dvořák, such as his *Slavonic Dances*, regularly incorporate folk music. He composed his final *New World Symphony* while he was director of the National Conservatory in New York City.

Antonín Dvořák

A portrait of Bohumil Hrabal

8 Bohumil Hrabal

The poetic author used to sit in the Old Town pub U Zlatého tygra (see p74), taking down the stories he heard there. He died falling from his hospital-room window in 1997.

9 Václav Havel

The former Czech president was known as a playwright and philosopher before he became a civil rights activist protesting the Warsaw Pact invasion in 1968 (see p43). His absurdist works and his fame helped draw international attention to the struggles of his country.

Czech-born writer Milan Kundera

10 Milan Kundera

Czechs have a love-hate relationship with their best-known contemporary author. Since his emigration to France in 1975, Kundera has had little to do with his native country, even writing his novels in French. His works convey a philosophical comic scepticism.

TOP 10 WORKS OF ART, MUSIC AND LITERATURE

Detail, Alfons Mucha's *Slav Epic*

1 Slav Epic
Art Nouveau master Alfons Mucha celebrates the Czech mythic past in this cycle of 20 large canvases.

2 The Castle
Kafka worked on this novel of social alienation while living in Prague Castle's Golden Lane (see p13).

3 The Good Soldier Švejk
Hašek was so effective in sending up the army and the Austro-Hungarian empire that Czechs still have a hard time taking authority seriously.

4 The Trial
The protagonist Joseph K. of Kafka's 1925 novel finds himself accused of a crime he did not commit.

5 R.U.R.
Karel Čapek's science-fiction play is a sometimes dark study of labour relations and social structures.

6 The Grandmother
Author Božena Němcová based the narrator in her 1855 novella *Babicka* on her own grandmother, from whom she heard many of these stories.

7 Vltava
Smetana's *Má vlast* (My homeland) is a set of six tone or symphonic poems celebrating Bohemia. The second, *Vltava*, follows the eponymous river's course.

8 New World Symphony
With his ninth symphony, composed in 1893, Dvořák incorporated the style of black American folk songs.

9 Disturbing the Peace
Havel meditates on Communism and the values underlying Central Europe's pursuit of democracy.

10 The Unbearable Lightness of Being
The novel is Kundera's non-linear tale of love, politics and the betrayals inherent in both.

ⓉⓄⓅ10 Museums and Galleries

1 National Gallery

Kinský Palace: MAP M3; Staroměstské náměstí 12 ▪ Sternberg Palace: MAP B2; Hradčanské náměstí 15 ▪ Salm Palace & Schwarzenberg Palace: MAP B2; Hradčanské náměstí 2 ▪ Open 10am–6pm Tue–Sun ▪ Adm ▪ www.ngprague.cz

The National Gallery's extensive art collection is spread throughout the city in six separate locations. Kinský Palace holds ancient and contemporary art from Asia; the Convent of St Agnes holds the medieval art collection (see pp34–5); Sternberg Palace boasts the Old Masters; the Trade Fair Palace has modern and contemporary art (see pp32–3); Salm Palace holds 19th-century art; and Schwarzenberg Palace has the gallery's collection of Baroque art.

National Gallery, Trade Fair Palace

2 National Museum

The country's leading natural history and ethnographic museum is closed until 2018, but the building still dominates Wenceslas Square. The annexe across the street holds rotating exhibitions (see p51 & p118).

3 Galerie Rudolfinum

MAP K2 ▪ Alšovo nábřeží 12 ▪ 227 059205 ▪ Open 10am–6pm Tue–Sun ▪ Adm ▪ www.galerie rudolfinum.cz

The "House of Artists" hosts a wide range of temporary exhibitions, each running for several months. It is always worth a visit, whatever aspect they are covering at the time.

Interior of the Smetana Museum

4 Smetana Museum

MAP J5 ▪ Novotného lávka 1 ▪ 221 082288 ▪ Open 10am–5pm Wed–Mon ▪ Adm ▪ www.nm.cz

Part of the National Museum, this grand Renaissance-style building, formerly owned by a water company, is a museum dedicated to the father of Czech music, Bedřich Smetana (see p44). Documents, letters, scores and instruments detailing his life and work are exhibited here.

5 Prague City Gallery

House at the Golden Ring: MAP M3; Týnská 6; open 10am–6pm Tue–Sun; adm ▪ House at the Stone Bell: MAP M3; Staroměstské náměstí 13; open 10am–8pm Tue–Sun; adm ▪ en.ghmp.cz

The House at the Golden Ring, the House at the Stone Bell (see p18) and the Old Town Hall (see pp20–21) have exhibitions of 19th- and 20th-century Czech art. The House at the Golden Ring also has a library of fine art books. Permanent exhibitions can be found in the Troja Château (see p126).

6 Montanelli Museum

MAP C2 ▪ Nerudova 13 ▪ 257 531220 ▪ Open noon–6pm daily ▪ Adm ▪ www.museum montanelli.com

This gallery of contemporary art holds the collection of the DrAK Foundation and a variety of imaginative modern works created by local and foreign artists. The gallery also holds educational programmes for children and runs regular guided tours in English.

Seder Plate, Jewish Museum

7 Jewish Museum

MAP L3 ■ Information & ticket centre: Maiselova 38/15 ■ Open 9am–6pm Sun–Fri (to 4:30pm in winter) ■ Adm ■ www.jewishmuseum.cz

The collection of Judaic art is perhaps the world's largest, while other exhibits present the lives and history of Jews in Bohemia and Moravia. The collection is spread out across the old synagogues of the Josefov quarter (see pp108–11).

8 National Technical Museum

MAP F1 ■ Kostelní 42 ■ Open 9am–5:30pm Tue–Fri, 10am–6pm Sat–Sun ■ Adm ■ www.ntm.cz

This is the ultimate how-things-work museum, with exhibitions on mining, metallurgy, telecommunications, printing, the measurement of time, chemistry, transport and astronomy.

Ask a guide to show you the coal mine in the basement.

9 Museum of Decorative Arts

MAP K3; 17. listopadu 2; 251 09311; open 10am–6pm Wed–Sun, until 7pm Tue; adm ■ House at the Black Madonna: MAP F3; Ovocný trh 19; open 10am–6pm Tue–Sun; www.upm.cz

The museum focuses on historical and contemporary crafts, applied arts and design. Exhibitions on Cubism are held at House at the Black Madonna, a classic Czech Cubist building.

Old trams, Public Transport Museum

10 Public Transport Museum

MAP A1 ■ Patočkova 4 ■ Open Apr–Nov: 9am–5pm Sat–Sun & holidays ■ Adm ■ www.dpp.cz/muzeum-mhd

A celebration of more than 100 years of Prague's transport systems. Exhibits range from horse-drawn carriages to the metro.

Exhibits at the National Technical Museum

TOP 10 Places of Worship

Stained glass at St Vitus Cathedral

1 St Vitus Cathedral

The current building, looming majestically over the castle complex, is a combination of architectural styles and took almost 600 years to complete. In days of old, the cathedral was the setting for spectacular Bohemian coronations conducted by Prague's archbishops. It is also the final resting place of the saints John of Nepomuk and Wenceslas, as well as scores of other Czech worthies (see pp16–17).

2 The Loreto

At the heart of this elaborate shrine to the Virgin Mary is the Santa Casa – a reproduction of the house where Mary received the Angel Gabriel. The Loreto treasury holds several priceless monstrances (open or transparent receptacles) and other religious artifacts (see pp26–7).

3 Old-New Synagogue

Prague's Orthodox Jewish community still holds services in this 13th-century synagogue – the oldest in Central Europe. Its curious name may come from the Hebrew *Al-Tenai*, meaning "with reservation". Legend has it that its stones will eventually have to be returned to Jerusalem, whence they came (see p30 & p109).

4 St Nicholas's Church, Malá Strana

The Malá Strana church clock tower and dome upstage its namesake across the river. The splendid Baroque sanctuary was meant to impress Catholic sceptics of the might of Rome (see p94).

5 Church of our Lady Victorious

This Baroque church contains the famed statue of the Infant Jesus of Prague. The wax baby doll is credited with miraculous powers. The resident Order of English Virgins look after the statue and change his clothes (see p95).

6 Basilica of St James

This is an active place of worship. The Baroque façade is awash with cherubs and scenes depicting episodes from the lives of saints Francis of Assisi, James and Antony of Padua. There is also a mummified arm hanging above the door inside (see p86).

Church of Our Lady before Týn

the latter was razed in 1867. The Conservative Jewish community holds services here. It also houses Jewish Museum exhibits, offices and a reference centre *(see p111)*.

9 Pinkas Synagogue

The names of nearly 80,000 Czech victims of the Holocaust cover the walls of this house adjacent to the Old Jewish Cemetery, as an emotive memorial *(see p31)*. The women's gallery was added in the 18th century *(see p111)*.

7 Church of Our Lady before Týn

MAP M3 ■ Staroměstské náměstí 14 ■ Open 10am–1pm & 3–5pm Tue–Sat, 10:30am–noon Sun

The Gothic towers of Týn loom over Old Town Square's houses. During the Counter-Reformation, the Jesuits melted down the gold Hussite chalice that stood between the towers and recast it as the Madonna seen today *(see p18)*.

8 Spanish Synagogue

The present Moorish building with its opulent interior replaced Prague's oldest synagogue after

10 Cathedral of Sts Cyril and Methodius

MAP E5 ■ Resslova 9 ■ Open Mar–Oct: 9am–5pm Tue–Sun; Nov–Feb: 9am–5pm Tue–Sat ■ Adm

The assassins of high-ranking Nazi *Reichsprotektor Obergruppenführer* Reinhard "The Hangman" Heydrich took refuge in this Eastern Orthodox cathedral *(see p117)* after the attack. A few days later, they were killed or committed suicide here. The Nazis

Romanesque portal

executed Bishop Gorazd, who had sheltered them.

The beautiful interior of the Spanish Synagogue

🔟 Communist Monuments

The soaring Žižkov TV Tower

1 Žižkov TV Tower
The city's most hated building among Praguers was built between 1985 and 1992, and was intended, so the rumour goes, to jam foreign radio signals or emit nefarious radiation. Its utilitarian design aside, however, the 216-m (709-ft) tower offers spectacular views of the city skyline on a clear day (see p125).

National Memorial on the Vítkov Hill

2 National Memorial on the Vítkov Hill
MAP B6 ▪ Vítkov Hill, Žižkov
▪ Open 10am–6pm Wed–Sun
After a failed attempt to embalm President Klement Gottwald after his death in 1953, the Communist government was forced to cremate their favoured leader. His ashes, as well as those of various other apparatchiks, were buried atop Vítkov Hill, behind the giant 1950 bronze equestrian statue of Jan Žižka. They were removed after the Velvet Revolution (see p43). Today the monument serves as a museum of Czech and Czechoslovak history (see p125).

3 Strahov Stadium
Prague Castle would fit inside this massive arena situated on Petřín Hill. Built in 1955 for the purposes of *spartakiáda* physical culture performances, this structure was the first concrete panel building in Czechoslovakia. Today, the stadium serves as a training centre for the AC Sparta football team. Some popular bands have also held performances here, much to the delight of local kids (see p38).

4 Letná Plinth
MAP E1 ▪ Letenské sady, Letná
Where sculptor V Karel Novák's giant metronome now swings there once stood a massive, 14,000-ton statue of Joseph Stalin – the largest in the world and visible from all over the city – backed by a queue of admiring citizens (see p124). Stalin's successor Nikita Khrushchev ordered the statue to be destroyed by a series of dramatic dynamite explosions in 1962. Pop star Michael Jackson launched his 1996 World Tour in Prague, unwisely erecting a statue of himself on the very same spot.

5 Congress Centre
Since its partial reconstruction in 2000, this has become one of the most modern congress centres in Europe. The excellent acoustics in the Congress Hall make this one of the best concert venues in the world, comparable to the famous halls of London, Montreal and Boston. The centre has capacity for close to 10,000 visitors and is used for a range of events (see p127).

6 Anděl Metro Station
MAP B6

In the reconstruction of the Anděl Centre, developers removed an epic mosaic tribute to the friendship between Moscow and Prague, but from the metro platforms below, you can still see frieze tributes to Soviet cosmonauts. Even if you're not riding the metro, you will need a standard ticket to access the platform.

7 Sbratření
MAP H3
■ Vrchlického sady

This 1947 bronze statue by Karel Pokorny recalls the Red Army's liberation of Prague in 1945: a grateful resistance fighter greets a Soviet foot soldier with a bunch of lilac and a, presumably brotherly, kiss. Inspired by a photograph taken in 1945 by Karel Ludwig, this is one of the few pro-Soviet monuments still standing in Prague.

Sbratření or Brotherhood

8 Czech Radio Building
MAP B6 ■ Vinohradská 12, Vinohrady ■ Closed to the public

Warsaw Pact tanks invaded the Czech capital in 1968 to put an end to Alexander Dubček's Prague Spring liberalization. Among those who paid for their resistance with their lives were Czech Radio journalists, who first broadcast the news that the nation was under attack. A plaque in front of the building honours their bravery.

9 Museum of Communism
This museum seeks to help visitors experience totalitarianism first hand through reproductions and genuine objects from the Communist era. The most chilling is the reconstructed interrogation room. Although locals might not agree, the tour is more fun than it sounds *(see p118)*.

10 New Building of the National Museum
MAP G5 ■ Vinohradská 1, New Town ■ Open 10am–6pm daily ■ Adm ■ www.nm.cz

From its construction in the 1970s until the country split into the Czech and Slovak republics in 1993, this unnamed building housed Czechoslovakia's Federal Assembly. It was home to Radio Free Europe from 1994 to 2009, and now hosts exhibitions of the National Museum *(see p46)*.

New Building of the National Museum

🔟 Parks and Gardens

Kampa Island separated from Malá Strana by the Čertovka (Devil's Canal)

1 Petřín Hill

The views from here are so beautiful that susceptible romantics have been known to spontaneously kiss passers-by, including the monks from Strahov monastery. In spring the views are at their best, as the orchards are in bloom (see pp38–9).

2 Vyšehrad

Far enough from the centre to be largely tourist-free, Vyšehrad is the perfect place to be alone with your thoughts. Sights include the Neo-Gothic Sts Peter and Paul Church, the graves of Dvořák and Smetana and reconstructed fortifications. However, visitors should be aware that there's very little shelter from inclement weather (see p123).

3 Wallenstein Garden

Albrecht von Wallenstein razed two dozen houses to make way for his expansive "backyard", which features a man-made lake. Among the garden's stranger elements is the grotto on the south wall, with stalactites imitating a limestone cave. The cries you hear all around you are the resident peacocks (see p79).

Wallenstein Garden's Sala Terrena

4 Kampa Island

Malá Strana residents love to sunbathe, sip wine and play frisbee on the island green of the Little Quarter in summer. However, they also like to smoke marijuana, beat drums well into the night and use the grass for a public dog toilet, so watch your step (see p94).

The pretty Vojanovy sady park

5 Vojanovy sady

Prague's oldest garden was founded in the 13th century. The fairy-tale park is home to peacocks, fruit trees and a heart-melting array of flowers (see p95).

6 Stromovka

King Přemysl Ottokar II established the royal hunting park here in 1266. A public garden since 1804, Stromovka is one of the city's largest parks. It has four ponds that are ideal for ice-skating in winter and duck-feeding in summer, and meandering paths that offer easy strolling (see p124).

9 Franciscan Garden

Stop here after pounding the pavements of Wenceslas Square and join the pensioners and office workers at lunch, quietly filling the benches behind the Church of Our Lady of the Snows (see p115).

10 Střelecký ostrov
MAP D4

Lose yourself watching the Vltava rush past this island, which gained its name from the archery competitions that were held here from the 15th century. Early risers can watch the sunrise strike the castle. In the summer there's a popular outdoor cinema and live-music stage here.

Prague Castle Royal Garden

7 Prague Castle Royal Garden

These formal gardens were laid out on the orders of the Habsburg king Ferdinand I in 1534 (see p101). After mulling over the Belvedere summer palace and the Communist-revised frescoes in the Ball Game Hall, slip down to the Stag Moat (see pp12–15).

8 South Gardens of Prague Castle

The spectacular views of Malá Strana from this series of gardens descending from Prague Castle can't fail to inspire. This really is the best way to conclude a day of sightseeing in Hradčany (see pp12–15).

The picturesque Střelecký ostrov

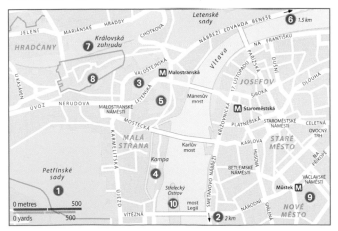

🔟 House Signs

The sign of the White Swan

1 The White Swan
Nerudova 49

Prague houses weren't given identifying numbers until 1770. Empress Maria Theresa was a great one for bringing the famed Habsburg trait of orderliness from Vienna to the banks of the Vltava. Before that, homes were known and located by a charming but confusing system of allegorical symbols. Although you can still find such emblematic addresses throughout the older parts of the city, Nerudova street in Malá Strana *(see p93)* has the highest concentration of house signs in the city. Originally many of them had local significance, although today much of their meaning has been lost. The White Swan is one of these, and probably originated as a golden goose (not to be confused with the downtown department store of the same name, Bílá Labut').

2 The Two Suns
Nerudova 47

This house was the birthplace of the much-loved Czech poet and author Jan Neruda (1834–91), after whom the street is named. Traditionally, this was the writers' and artists' area of Prague, and Neruda conveyed the Bohemian atmosphere of Malá Strana in his work. The connection continues today with the quarter's many small art galleries and craft shops.

The Two Suns

3 The Golden Key
Nerudova 27

Castle goldsmiths, such as the ones who worked at this house in the 17th century, paid fees to the city, unlike their colleagues who lived in the castle's Golden Lane *(see p13)*. As such, they were entitled to advertise their wares, as preserved today in this building's façade.

The statue at the Red Lamb

4 The Red Lamb
Nerudova 11

One of the street's more unlikely symbols, the scarlet sheep adorning this façade has a significance so arcane, not even the current house owner can explain it. Not that it matters – it remains in place as one of the city's many charming idiosyncrasies.

5 The Golden Wheel
Nerudova 28

This house symbol may have had something to do with alchemy – the wheel represents a stage in the *magnum opus*, the process by which the base metal lead was purportedly turned into gold. Modern-day alchemists are usually more interested in the meditative aspects of the art, however.

Beautifully crafted house sign indicating the Three Fiddles

6 The Three Fiddles
Nerudova 12

They say a demonic trio screeches on their instruments here on moonlit nights. The house was home to a family of violin-makers in the early 18th century, and the sign advertised their trade. Like many of the other buildings on this street, it is now home to a restaurant.

7 The Three Lilies
Nerudova 15

Although their image no longer adorns the façade, the three flowers remain atop the house. The house also lends its name to a feverish tale of passion and thunderstorms by Jan Neruda. Many of the author's tales were set in houses such as this one.

8 The Devil
Nerudova 4

Lucifer pops up as a cuddly character on houses all over town and in local legend, more a folksy trickster than a sinister prince of darkness. At this house he'll tempt you to dine at the Restaurant U Čerta.

The Devil

9 The Green Lobster
Nerudova 43

Who knows what they were thinking when they hung the crustacean above their door – probably trying to keep up with the neighbours at the Pendant Parsnip at No. 39.

10 St Wenceslas's Horse
Staroměstské náměsti 16

Seen on the façade of Štorch House at the Old Town Square (see p18), this is a tribute both to the patron saint of Bohemia and the blacksmiths who shod horses bound for the castle.

The image of St Wenceslas's Horse

🔟 Off the Beaten Track

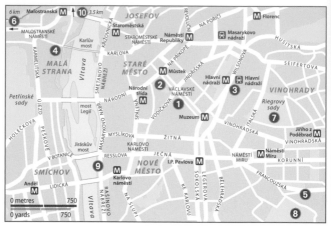

1 David Černý's Upside-Down Horse Statue

MAP N6 ■ Štěpánská 61 ■ 224 225440 ■ Open 9am–10pm daily ■ www.lucerna.cz

Works by Czech installation artist David Černý can be seen around the city, but this hanging statue of St Wenceslas astride an upside-down horse in the central passage of the Palác Lucerna is worth a special look and a laugh. It is a gentle parody of the pompous horse statue at the top of Wenceslas Square.

2 Cubist Lamppost

MAP M6 ■ Jungmannovo náměstí

The city of Prague was a hotbed of architectural experimentation in the 20th century, enthusiastically embracing the application of Cubist design concepts to all manner of buildings and objects, including – apparently – lampposts. The only one of its kind in the world, this street light can be found on a quiet corner between Václavské náměstí and Jungmannovo náměstí.

Cubist Lamppost

3 Fantova Kavárna

MAP H4 ■ Wilsonova 80 ■ 778 749662 ■ www.cafecoffeeday.cz

Prague's main train station, Hlavní nádraží, was once a beautiful building. For proof, head upstairs from the grand concourse to admire the opulent 1909 Art Nouveau Fantova Kavárna, named after the station's architect. The ambience and the beautiful interiors of the renovated station can be appreciated while sipping coffee at the café.

Upside-Down Horse Statue

Previous pages View from castle over Prague and St Nicholas's Church, Malá Strana

Karel Zeman Museum

7 Riegrovy Sady
MAP H5

This sprawling park, partly designed in the style of an English garden, offers plenty of room to spread a blanket and admire views out over the Old Town with Prague Castle in the distance.

4 Karel Zeman Museum
MAP D3 ■ Saský dvůr, Malá Strana ■ 724 341091 ■ Open 10am–7pm daily ■ www.muzeum karlazemana.cz

This hands-on, interactive museum focuses on the work of renowned Czech film-maker Karel Zeman, who directed several noteworthy Czech fantasy films, including *The Fabulous World of Jules Verne* and *The Fabulous Baron Munchausen*.

8 Grebovka
MAP B6 ■ Havlíčkovy sady 2188 ■ Open 10am–10pm daily ■ www.pavilongrebovka.cz

Vinohrady was once covered by vineyards (that's what the name means). This pleasant gazebo in a park south of Náměstí Míru is all that's left, but it is still a wonderful place to spend a sunny afternoon sipping wine in the open air.

5 Krymská
MAP C6

Prague's nascent hipster scene is thriving along this pleasantly dilapidated street in the district of Vršovice. There are several good cafés and bars, where modern trends and old Prague clash to fascinating effect.

9 Náplavka
MAP E6 ■ New Town

The Vltava's eastern bank south of the National Theatre has come into its own as the go-to summer venue, with everything from music festivals to farmers' markets (see p79).

6 Divoká Šárka
MAP A5 ■ Open May–Aug daily

This expansive nature reserve offers a touch of wilderness within a short tram ride of the centre. There are rugged rock formations, deep forests and even a refreshing stream-fed swimming pool during the summer months.

10 Hotel International
MAP B5 ■ Koulova 15 ■ www.internationalprague.cz

Despite spending 40 years under Communism, Prague has little architecture to show for it. This stunning Socialist-Realist palace – a 1950s gift from the Soviet Union – is an impressive reminder. Check out the period-piece lobby decor.

Hotel International

🔟 Haunted Places

The atmospheric interior of Mysteriae Pragensis museum

1 Mysteriae Pragensis
MAP D3 ■ Mostecká 18
■ www.muzeumpovesti.cz

Uncover old Prague's most famous mysteries and legends in this museum exploring the city's ghosts and stories. The atmospheric cellar has a replica of some of old Prague's streets, while the ground floor offers more traditional exhibits that explain the background to the legends. All of the material on show is based on authentic records.

Representation of the Golem

2 Turk in Ungelt
Among the merchants who lived in the Týn settlement behind the Church of Our Lady (see p49) was a Turkish immigrant. When his betrothed ran off and married another, he flew into a rage and chopped her head off. He is said to wander around the Ungelt courtyard carrying the decapitated head.

3 One-Armed Thief
The story of the thief who sought to steal jewels from a statue of the Madonna in the Basilica of St James (see p48), claims that the stony Virgin seized him by the arm and local butchers had to cut him loose. According to some, the thief still haunts the church asking visitors to help him fetch his arm, which hangs from the wall inside.

4 The Golem
It is said that the Prague rabbi Judah Loew (see p110) created a clay automaton to defend the Jews of the Prague ghetto. When the creature ran amok one day, Loew was forced to deactivate him and stash him in the attic of the Old-New Synagogue (see p30 & p109).

5 The Iron Man
Believing his fiancée to be untrue, a knight called off their wedding. After she drowned herself in grief, he realized his mistake and hanged himself. Every 100 years he appears in Platnéřská street to find a young virgin who will free him by talking to him for at least an hour.

6 The Drowned Man
When the bicycle was all the rage in the late 19th century, young Boběř Říma stole one and rode it into the river. If a soggy young fellow tries to sell you a bike near the Old Town end of Charles Bridge, just keep walking.

7 Emaus Devil

In an attempt to bedevil the monks at the Emaus Monastery *(see p117)*, Satan worked there as a cook and seasoned their food with pepper and other spices. To this day, Czech cuisine has few piquant flavours.

8 Werewolf

Apparently, the gamekeeper of Rudolf II became so enamoured with the wolves that roamed the castle's Stag Moat that he became one himself. Nowadays, he takes the form of a large dog and tends to chase cyclists, joggers and tourists when the whim takes him, so keep looking over your shoulder.

Woodcut (1512) of a werewolf attack

9 Drahomíra

St Wenceslas's mother was, by all accounts, an unpleasant woman. She killed her mother-in-law and might have done in her son, too, but the gates of hell swallowed her up before she could act. She sometimes wheels through Loretánská náměstí in a fiery carriage.

10 The Mad Barber

When a local barber forsook his home and family after he became caught up in alchemical pursuits, his daughters ended up in a brothel and his wife killed herself. He is said to haunt Karlova and Liliova streets, hoping to return to his honest profession and make amends.

TOP 10 FALSE STORIES

The brass cross on Charles Bridge

1 John of Nepomuk Died on Charles Bridge
Nepomuk was already dead when he was thrown over the side *(see pp22–3)*.

2 Vyšehrad Castle
Vyšehrad *(see p123)* was the first seat of power, but its importance has been inflated by legend.

3 Alchemists Lived in Golden Lane
Alchemists tended to live on credit in houses in town.

4 Czechs are Believers
According to the last census, almost 59 per cent of Czechs declared themselves to be atheists.

5 Jan Masaryk Committed Suicide
In 1948 the foreign minister was found dead in front of Černín Palace, having "fallen" from a window, according to the Communists.

6 There's Only One Bud
The town of České Budějovice (Budweis in German) was producing beer before the US brewer, but didn't register its copyright on the name.

7 The Danube Flows Through Prague
It's incredible how many visitors think the Danube flows through the Czech capital. The river here is the Vltava.

8 Absinth Will Make You Crazy
The amount of wormwood in the drink is negligible.

9 Czechs and Slovaks are the Same Nation
Despite claims that they form a single nation, the languages and mentalities are different.

10 Prague is the New Left Bank
After the Velvet Revolution, some wag proclaimed Prague "the Paris of the 90s", due to the number of expats.

🔟 Eccentric Prague

Mesoamerican-style doorway at Choco-Story chocolate museum

① Choco-Story

MAP M4 ■ Celetná 10
■ Open 10am–7pm daily ■ Adm
■ www.choco-story-praha.cz

This chocoholic's delight is based on the well-known Chocolate Museum in Bruges, Belgium, and showcases the 2,600-year history of this delicacy, from the discovery of cocoa to today's modern production methods. Visitors will also get the chance to learn the secret of producing silky chocolate and to sample products made on the spot.

② Museum of Torture

MAP M4 ■ Celetná 12
■ Open 10am–10pm daily (to 8pm in winter) ■ Adm ■ www.museum tortury.cz

If you can't quite grasp how these grisly instruments work, the helpful illustrations should make their operation painfully clear. Approximately 100 implements of pain and dozens of etchings from all over Europe are on display, along with explanations in four languages.

Neck trap

③ Pragulic

MAP L6 ■ Národní třída 417/35
■ 725 314930 ■ www.pragulic.cz

This unusual social enterprise enables you to experience the world from the perspective of homeless people, challenge stereotypes and gain insight into their daily life. Walking tours are organized by guides among the homeless and visitors can choose between short 2-hour tours or a 24-hour one.

④ Grévin Wax Museum

MAP M4 ■ Celetná 15 ■ 226 776776 ■ Open 10am–7pm daily (to 9pm Sat) ■ Adm ■ www.grevin-praha.com

Walk among lifelike waxworks of famous people from history and the present day and have your photograph taken with them. The exhibition is divided thematically and includes wax figures of Mozart, Obama, George Clooney and Brad Pitt, among other famous personalities.

⑤ Sex Machines Museum

MAP L4 ■ Melantrichova 18
■ Open 10am–11pm daily ■ Adm
■ www.sexmachinesmuseum.com

An exhibition in a slightly different sense, this is one show definitely not for kids. The museum traces the history of instruments for sexual gratification, from their origins to the modern day. While not entirely without cultural merit, the overall package is rather bizarre. There is also, predictably, a gift shop.

6 Marionette Don Giovanni

Mozart premiered his opera *Don Giovanni* in 1787 at Prague's Estates Theatre *(see p67)*. Of the two marionette homages to the city's favourite opera, the better production takes place at the National Marionette Theatre *(see p67)*. The technique of the puppeteers is so masterful, you'll leave looking for strings attached to passers-by. A true Prague experience.

National Marionette Theatre

7 Křižík Fountain

MAP B5 ■ Výstaviště, Holešovice

Every evening during the summer, the fountain's 50 pumps, 3,000 water jets and more than 1,200 lights put on a visually dizzying display of hydro-mechanic choreography. The musical accompaniment ranges from classical to heavy metal to Disney film tunes. Productions have included live folk dance troupes and a melodrama based on James Bond plots *(see p124)*.

8 The Magic Flute

Mozart's last opera, written in 1791, this magical fairy-tale *singspiel* is a classic reimagined in a new playful concept of figures and puppetry at the National Marionette Theatre *(see p67)*. The story of Prince Tamino and Princess Pamina is full of humour and enchanting fantasy and continues to entertain viewers as it has done for over 200 years.

9 McGee's Ghost Tours

MAP M3 ■ Týnská 7
■ www.mcgeesghosttours.com

Whether you are a believer, a sceptic, interested in the unexplained or simply looking for an entertaining evening, guides will take you through narrow lanes and cobbled alleys to the ancient churches and monuments, where you will hear about alchemists, murderers and the other unfortunate souls who lived there.

10 Musicals

Divadlo Broadway: MAP N5; Na Příkopě 31 ■ Hudební Divadlo Karlín: MAP K4; Křižíkova 10

The Czech love of musicals knows no limits, except perhaps the number of performers willing to take part in the latest musical at locations around town. It began with *Romeo a Julie*, proceeded to a romping *Monte Cristo* and is still going strong with *The Three Musketeers*, *Hamlet*, *Dracula 2015* and *The Addams Family*. Check theatre websites for details.

Multicoloured jets of water choreographed to music at the Křižík Fountain

Children's Attractions

Castle-like entrance of the Petřín Hill Mirror Maze

1 Mirror Maze

The warped mirrors lining the walls here are great fun for making faces, pointing fingers at distended bellies and elongated bodies and giggling hysterically, whatever your age. For older children interested in a bit of gore and history combined, the battle-scene diorama is another of the many attractions on Petřín Hill *(see pp38–9)*.

Czech puppet

2 Swan Feeding
MAP D4

Grab a bag of seeds and head to the riverbank. Střelecký ostrov (island) is an ideal spot to watch these graceful white birds dip their necks in the water to catch the morsels, much to children's delight. Take care that little feet don't go into the water and mud, however, and make sure that fingers don't inadvertently get snapped in the feeding frenzy. Good for all seasons.

3 Puppet Shows

Puppetry is a long-standing Czech tradition, and late afternoon shows will keep your children entertained for up to an hour. There's enough action that younger folk usually don't mind not understanding the libretto or narration. Weekend presentations of well-known fairy tales at the National Marionette Theatre can fill up quickly, so book in advance *(see p67)*.

4 Gargoyle-Spotting

This is rather addictive. Give the little ones their first taste finding faces on St Vitus Cathedral *(see pp16–17)* and they'll have their heads pointed upwards for days. In addition to gargoyles, train your kids to spot the innumerable statues, house signs *(see pp54–5)* and strange faces that adorn arches, cornices and gateways all over the city. Just take care that they don't get stiff necks or stumble on uneven pavement surfaces.

Gargoyle, St Vitus Cathedral

5 White Tower

MAP C2 ■ Zlatá ulička, Prague Castle ■ Open Apr–Oct: 9am–5pm, Nov–Mar: 9am–4pm ■ Adm

This is an entertaining spot at Prague Castle. Here kids can shoot a real crossbow, pick out their favourite suit of armour and imagine the grisly goings-on in the torture chamber. They'll have no trouble negotiating the low, narrow passages, but the adults with them might.

6 Historic Tram No. 91

MAP B5 ■ Apr–Oct: noon–5pm Sat & Sun ■ www.dpp.cz

The old-fashioned streetcar runs a circuit around the city in about 30 minutes. A friendly conductor will take your Kč35 fare and you can hop on and off at any stop on the route, including Malostranská and the National Theatre (see p66) – very handy when you can't face walking another step. For those who are planning ahead, the end station is Výstaviště, scene of more excitement.

7 Výstaviště

In addition to Křižík Fountain, the Prague exhibition grounds are home to the Lunapark carnival: ferris wheels, rollercoasters and other similar rides will toss and turn the kids for hours, and, if they can still stomach it, there's even candy floss (cotton candy). The fun begins in March and carries on through the warmer summer months (see p124).

8 Black Light Theatre

MAP K4 ■ Divadlo Ta Fantastika: Karlova 8

There is an abundance of black-light shows at theatres around the Old Town (see p66), but the best one is at Divadlo Ta Fantastika. So long as the youngsters don't mind strange images suddenly popping out of the dark, the brilliant displays should keep them mesmerized.

9 Boat Trips

While adults might enjoy the old-fashioned (and more romantic) rowing boats, children will prefer the splashing, pedalling action of the miniature paddleboats that travel up and down the Vltava. Numerous vendors rent boats and sell tickets in the vicinity of the National Theatre (see p66). Take all the usual precautions that no one goes overboard, accidentally or otherwise.

Sightseeing boats on the Vltava

10 Prague Zoo

MAP B5 ■ U Trojského zámku 120, Troja ■ www.zoopraha.cz

Prague Zoo is located on a rocky slope north of the centre overlooking the right bank of the Vltava. Founded in 1924, it is now home to about 4,700 animals representing more than 670 species, 140 of them extremely rare in the wild.

A young orangutan at Prague Zoo

🔟 Performing Arts Venues

Graceful exterior of the State opera

1 State Opera
MAP G4 ■ Wilsonova 4 ■ 224 901448 ■ www.narodni-divadlo.cz

Set at the top of Wenceslas Square next to the National Museum, the Státní opera, currently undergoing renovation, offers a repertoire heavy on Italian and Viennese favourites.

2 Divadlo Archa
MAP P3 ■ Na Poříčí 26 ■ www.divadloarcha.cz

Prague's premiere venue for avant-garde music, dance and movement theatre. David Byrne and Compagnie Pál Frenák have performed here.

3 Hybernia
MAP P4 ■ Náměstí Republiky 4 ■ www.hybernia.eu

Housed in a former monastery, this musical theatre opened in 2006 with the musical *Golem*. It hosts a range of cultural events.

The foyer at the Ponec theatre

4 Ponec
MAP C6 ■ Husitská 24a, Žižkov ■ www.divadloponec.cz

This contemporary dance and movement theatre space, opened in 2001, has all aspects covered, from top international dance acts to workshops for young talent.

5 Smetana Hall
MAP P3 ■ Náměstí Republiky 5 ■ 222 002336 ■ www.fok.cz

The glorious Art Nouveau Smetana Hall at the Municipal House is home to the Prague Symphony Orchestra (Fok). The spring music festival *(see p80)* traditionally opens here with Smetana's *Má vlast (see p45)*.

6 Laterna Magika
MAP K6 ■ Národní třída 4 ■ www.narodni-divadlo.cz

This company was the main proponent behind black-light theatre, a genre in which black-clad actors manipulate objects, working against a black background.

Performance at the Laterna Magika

7 National Theatre
The Národní divadlo curtain first went up for Smetana's *Libuše* in 1883; you can still see this or other Czech operas on the same stage. Go to a performance, if only to appreciate the artistic work that went into creating the theatre *(see p116)*.

8 Rudolfinum
MAP K2 ■ Alšovo nábřeží 12 ■ www.rudolfinum.cz

The Rudolfinum is home to the Czech Philharmonic. During World War II, the Nazis sought to remove Felix Mendelssohn from the statues on the roof, but inadvertently ousted Richard Wagner instead *(see p46)*.

The 18th-century Estates Theatre

(9) Estates Theatre
MAP M4 ▪ Ovocný trh 1
▪ www.narodni-divadlo.cz

Stavovské divadlo is well known as the venue where Mozart's *Don Giovanni* saw its first performance. It was also the first Czech-language playhouse in what was then a largely German-speaking city. The productions occasionally leave something to be desired, but if you don't see the *Don* here, then where?

(10) National Marionette Theatre
MAP L3 ▪ Žatecká 1 ▪ www.mozart.cz

The National Theatre's puppet stage represents the pinnacle of this much-loved genre, staging wonderful productions of Czech fairy tales and other child-pleasing shows (in Czech). They have the best Beatles tribute in town and a marionette version of *Don Giovanni* (see p63).

***Don Giovanni* marionette show**

TOP 10 CHURCHES FOR MUSIC RECITALS

St Nicholas's Church, Old Town

1 St Nicholas's Church, Old Town
The Old Town church hosts chamber music recitals twice daily *(see p87)*.

2 Convent of St Agnes
This medieval convent regularly holds recitals *(see pp34–5)*.

3 St Nicholas's Church, Malá Strana
Appreciate the Malá Strana church's Baroque grandeur at a concert of sacred music *(see p94)*.

4 Basilica of St James
This active house of worship regularly invites the general public to hear its organ *(see p86)*.

5 Mirror Chapel
The Baroque chamber of the Clementinum hosts string quartets and other small ensembles *(see p86)*.

6 St Martin in the Wall
MAP L6 ▪ Martinská 8
Organ and other recitals are on the bill at this Gothic church, which was once part of the Old Town defences.

7 Spanish Synagogue
The ornate 1880 organ figures in the sacred music concerts held in this opulent synagogue *(see p111)*.

8 St George's Basilica
Choral and string recitals present the greatest works of Mozart, Beethoven and other composers *(see p12)*.

9 Church of Sts Simon and Jude
MAP L1 ▪ U Milosrdných
Catch an ensemble of the Prague Symphony Orchestra players in this Renaissance sanctuary.

10 St Kajetan Church
MAP C2 ▪ Nerudova 22
This magnificent church regularly holds concerts of Bach, Mozart or Brahms.

🔟 Clubs

The glittering bar at Radost FX

① Radost FX
The most chic disco in Prague pushes the limits with parties so hedonistic you wonder if there isn't a law against them. Hip-hop, funk and disco are the prevalent flavours on the dance floor. The vegetarian café upstairs is open until 4am. During peak lunch and dinner hours, it can be very hard to find a seat (see p119).

② Roxy
MAP N2 ▪ Dlouhá 33
▪ www.roxy.cz
Located in the Old Town, this former cinema is a must for fans of jungle and dub. Parties continue well into the morning, much to the dismay of the neighbours. Such live acts as the Asian Dub Foundation take the stage when it's not occupied by DJs or an experimental theatre production. A portion of Roxy's proceeds goes towards funding Prague's Linhart Foundation, a non-profit organization whose aim is to promote contemporary art (see p89).

View from the DJ booth at Roxy

③ Palác Akropolis
MAP C6 ▪ Kubelíkova 27,
Žižkov ▪ www.palacakropolis.com
In addition to being at the heart of Prague's indie and world-music scene, the Palác Akropolis hosts the likes of Ani Difranco, Apollo 440 and Transglobal Underground. The small, smoky Divadelní bar is the hippest, hosting Prague's best DJs. On the ground-floor level is a café and Czech restaurant. On a more cultural note, this is also the best venue in town to hear contemporary Romany music from such local acts as Alom or Věra Bílá and Kale.

Stylish interior of SaSaZu

④ SaSaZu
MAP C5 ▪ Bubenské nábřeží
306 ▪ www.sasazu.com
One of the largest entertainment spaces in Prague, capable of accommodating up to 2,500 guests, SaSaZu has welcomed many well-known performers from all around the world, including British singer Lily Allen, Dutch DJ Tiësto, American rapper Pitbull and pop band One Republic. The hip restaurant offers excellent food from East Asia and boasts a Michelin Bib Gourmand.

Live music at U Malého Glena

⑤ U Malého Glena
MAP C3 ■ Karmelitská 23
■ www.malyglen.cz

The shoebox-sized cellar at "Little Glenn's" has to be Prague's smallest jazz venue. The music ranges from African-inspired drumming to blues to modern jazz, and most of it is of a high standard. Upstairs is a café where you can get reasonable food and brunch at weekends. The club is run by the same people who operate Bohemia Bagel (see p98).

⑥ Karlovy lázně
MAP J5 ■ Novotného lávka, Smetanovo nábřeží 198 ■ www.karlovylazne.cz

The former public bathhouse, just 100 m (330 ft) from Charles Bridge, was converted into a dance club in the late 1990s. You can still admire the original tiles along the corridors and the splendid mosaic murals. Drained of water, the pools now serve as the dance floors (see p89).

⑦ Mecca
MAP C5 ■ U Průhonu 3, Holešovice ■ www.mecca.cz

The proprietors of Mecca have turned this former factory in the Holešovice warehouse district into a giant dance-and-dining emporium. The food is nouvelle cuisine, the crowd trendy and the parties cool. A little off the beaten track – take a taxi – but worth it. The restaurant serves food until 2am.

⑧ Blue Light Bar
MAP C3 ■ Josefská 1, Malá Strana ■ www.bluelightbar.cz

This is the place to go if you find yourself in Malá Strana looking for a last drink. Though the sign out front proclaims this a jazz bar, don't be fooled by appearances. This rowdy, raucous cocktail bar starts to fill up at around 10pm; the party usually lasts until 3am. There's a cramped bar up front and a couple of rooms with tables towards the back.

⑨ Rock Café
MAP L6 ■ Národní 20
■ www.rockcafe.cz

Prague's music scene is teeming with so-called "revival bands", most of whom take the stage here with tributes to everyone from Jimi Hendrix to Sadé. There are also several bars, an internet café and a screening room where you can watch films of various past rock concerts.

⑩ Lucerna Music Bar
MAP N6 ■ Vodičkova 36
■ www.musicbar.cz

Local "big-beat" acts are the mainstay at this music bar, but it occasionally hosts big names in jazz such as Maceo Parker, as well as where-are-they-now relics (an adjoining venue, the Velký sál, or large hall, hosts bigger acts such as Wynton Marsalis). The club's 1980s and 1990s night is one of the biggest dance parties in town (see p119).

Dance floor of the Lucerna Music Bar

Restaurants

1 Kampa Park

Consistently rated Prague's best restaurant, chic Kampa Park has an unparalleled riverside location and an outstanding menu with influences from all over the world *(see p99)*. It is part of the Kampa Group, which has another excellent restaurant in the city.

2 La Degustation (Bohême Bourgeoise)

MAP N2 ▪ Haštalská 18 ▪ 222 311234 ▪ Ⓚ Ⓚ Ⓚ

One of the most intriguing dining experiences in Prague, with chefs offering a choice of three seven-course taster menus that unfold over a three-hour period. The restaurant boasts a Michelin star.

The modern interiors of V Zátiší

3 V Zátiší

MAP K5 ▪ Liliová 1 ▪ 222 221155 ▪ Ⓚ Ⓚ Ⓚ

Prague was introduced to fine dining at this small Bethlehem Square restaurant. The *dégustation* menu – a selection of tasters – brings out the kitchen's best and pairs it with select Moravian wines. The seafood is so good you'll forget you're in a land-locked country.

La Degustation (Bohême Bourgeoise)

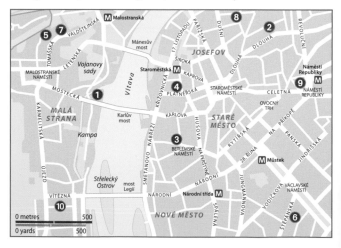

4 La Finestra in Cucina
MAP K4 ▪ Platnéřská 13 ▪ 222 325325 ▪ ⓀⓀⓀ

Traditional and delicious Italian cuisine is served in a cosy setting. The open kitchen allows diners to watch the chef as he prepares their meal, and an impressive selection of French wines is on offer.

5 Terasa U Zlaté studně
MAP C2 ▪ U Zlaté studně 4 ▪ 257 533322 ▪ ⓀⓀⓀ

Dining atop the hotel of the same name (see p141), guests of "At the Golden Well" may think they've died and gone to heaven. The classic Continental cuisine matches the view – but only just. The dining room is tiny, so make sure you make your reservations well in advance.

6 Alcron
MAP G4 ▪ Štěpánská 40 ▪ 222 820410 ▪ Closed Sun ▪ ⓀⓀⓀ

Seafood is the speciality at this Michelin-starred restaurant of the Radisson (see p141), but chef Roman Paulus is happy to prepare almost any dish. Just make your request as he does the rounds of this small Art Deco lounge. If the dining room is full, try La Rotonde, which is just across the foyer. After dinner, enjoy cocktails and some great live jazz in the Be Bop bar.

The tiny Art Deco-style Alcron

7 Pálffy Palác
Enjoy the romantic ambience of one of the most famous Baroque buildings in town. Nestled in Prague Castle's imposing walls, this fine dining establishment offers palatial surroundings and an expansive, changing menu of traditional Czech and European cuisine. A memorable dining experience with impeccable service (see p99). If you can't get a table, choose a takeaway dish from the Pálffy Delicatessen menu.

A dish of quail served at Field

8 Field
MAP M1 ▪ U Milosrdných 12 ▪ 222 316999 ▪ ⓀⓀⓀ

Prague's best example of farm-to-table dining, with an emphasis on free-range poultry and livestock, local ingredients and simple presentation. The main courses are built around unusual but traditional bases like smoked beef tongue and rabbit. Reservations are a must.

9 Plzeňská restaurace Obecní dům
MAP P3 ▪ Náměstí Republiky 5 ▪ 222 002770 ▪ ⓀⓀ

It may be a bit touristy, but it's fun nevertheless. Gorgeous tiled mosaics of bucolic Bohemians cover the walls while an accordionist rolls out the Beer-Barrel Polka almost nonstop. The traditional food and beer are good and fairly priced.

10 Ichnusa Botega Bistro
MAP D4 ▪ Plaská 5 ▪ 605 375012 ▪ ⓀⓀ

The owner has brought a piece of his native Sardinia to Prague, so expect big appetizer plates of thinly sliced dried ham, prosciutto and cheeses, followed by mains of fresh fish, pork and pasta. The wines are home-made and also brought in from Sardinia. Reservations advised.

For a key to restaurant price ranges see p91

🔟 Prague Dishes

Czech guláš with bread *knedlíky*

1 Guláš
Not quite as spicy as its Hungarian cousin, Czech goulash is essentially a rich beef stew minus the vegetables. Don't even think of ordering it without *knedlíky* (dumplings) on the side. Beef forms part of the standard recipe for this staple dish, but you can sometimes find goulash using venison, pork and even vegetarian variants.

2 Pivní sýr
"Beer cheese" is marinated in ale until semi-soft. It is best enjoyed spread on dark sourdough bread and sprinkled with chopped onions.

3 Knedlíky
These doughy dumplings are the side dish of choice for many gravy-laden Czech dishes. In addition to the savoury varieties, made with bread, potato or bacon *(špekové)*, *knedlíky* also come stuffed with fruit *(ovocné knedlíky)*, the most popular variety being plums *(švestkové)*.

4 Svíčková na smetaně
This is goulash's sweet cousin: slices of pot-roasted beef tenderloin are served in a carrot-sweetened cream sauce, topped with a dollop of whipped cream and cranberries. Apparently, this was one of President Václav Havel's favourite dishes. Like goulash, it's unthinkable to eat it without the *knedlíky* to mop up the sauce.

Rounds of *Olomoucké syrečky*

5 Olomoucké syrečky
Also known as *Olomoucké tvarůžky*, these small cheese rounds immediately announce themselves by their pungent aroma. Eat them as a snack or light lunch, accompanied by beer, bread and onions.

6 Utopence
These pickled sausages, slightly sour, fatty and always piled high with pickled onions, are an ideal accompaniment to the local beer, as a lunchtime or early evening snack.

A dish of *ovocné knedlíky* dumplings stuffed with strawberries

7 Smažený sýr
Comparable to fried mozzarella sticks, this battered block of deep-fried mild cheese is usually served with French fries *(hranolky)* and a tangy tartare sauce. As with much of Czech cuisine, try not to think about the cholesterol.

8 Vepřoknedlozelo
This name is the shortened version for *vepřové, knedlíky a zelí* – pork, dumplings and sauerkraut. Heavy on fat but big on flavour, this is true Czech soul food. Order it instead of goulash and you'll impress your waiter with how acclimatized you are, assuming you pronounce it right, of course.

9 Halušky
The Germans call these plump little noodles *Spaetzle*. They are included in the Czech culinary canon as a nod to nearby Slovakia, from where they originate and with whom Bohemia has shared so much recent history. You can order them *s zelím* (with sauerkraut) or *s bryndzou* (with a creamy, sharp cheese). The dish is a filling and cheap Eastern European alternative to pasta.

Halušky

10 Rohlíky
The workhorse of the Prague diet, these ubiquitous banana-shaped bread rolls are served up to accompany the main meal at breakfast, lunch and dinner. Dip them in soft cheese or your dish's sauce, spread them with pâté or order them with a hot-dog on nearly every street corner.

TOP 10 CZECH BEERS

Staropramen beer

1 Staropramen
The hometown favourite has a light, fruity flavour. Brewed in the Smíchov district, its popularity owes as much to marketing as it does to local pride.

2 Pilsner Urquell
The best-known Czech beer on the international market comes from the town of Plzeň, 80 km (50 miles) southwest of Prague. It has a strong, hoppy flavour.

3 Krušovice
Rudolf II established the Krušovice brewery, which produces this sweet and somewhat flat beer. Try the syrupy dark *(tmavé)* variety.

4 Budvar
Brewed in the town of České Budějovice, the beer is no relation to the American Budweiser *(see p61)*.

5 Velkopopovický Kozel
This strong, smooth beer is well worth seeking out – some consider it the world's finest.

6 Bakalář
Countryside lager brewed in Rakovník, 50 km (30 miles) west of Prague.

7 Gambrinus
Brewed by Pilsner Urquell, this is the best-selling beer in the country. Try the 11° variety.

8 Bernard
This unpasteurized beer has a distinct, bittersweet flavour and a hoppy aroma.

9 Únětické
This popular microbrew from a small family-run brewery can be hard to find but worth the effort.

10 Svijany
The brewery produces highly rated dark and light beers, including the popular Svijanský Máz pale lager.

🔟 Bars and Kavárnas

Knights' Hall at U Fleků

1 U Fleků

The city's oldest brewing pub, dating to 1499, U Fleků is famous for its delicious dark lager and somewhat more than modest prices. Despite what anyone might tell you, the Becherovka shots are not complimentary and the rounds will keep coming until you say *"ne"* five times. Very popular with tourists, and not without reason *(see p120)*.

2 Café Slavia
MAP J6 ■ Národní třída 1
■ 224 218493 ■ www.cafeslavia.cz

Across from the National Theatre and on a busy river thoroughfare, Café Slavia with its 1930s Art Deco interior is a famous literary café. Enjoy a coffee and dessert at the end of the day or after a night at the theatre, admiring the view of the riverside and Prague Castle.

3 U Zlatého tygra
MAP L4 ■ Husova 17
■ 222 221111 ■ No credit cards
■ www.uzlatehotygra.cz

This legendary pub, famed as the haunt of the late writer Bohumíl Hrabal *(see p45)*, serves the finest mug of Pilsner Urquell in the city. Regulars were indifferent when Václav Havel brought Bill Clinton in for a cold glass when they were both serving presidents, so don't expect them to take much interest in you.

4 Pivovarský dům
MAP F6 ■ Lípová 15
■ 296 216666 ■ www.pivovarsky
dum.com

Excellent, rustic Czech fare. The house brewmaster is always concocting new flavours for his drinks, such as coffee lager or champagne ale. You can also see the fermenting vats slowly making beer, if the process of brewing interests you.

Exterior of Pivovarský dům

5 Tretter's

MAP L2 ▪ V Kolkovně 3
▪ 224 811165 ▪ www.tretters.cz

This is Prague's – and perhaps Europe's – best cocktail bar. It may look like a Jazz Age time capsule, but Tretter's is actually a relative newcomer, and highly welcome at that. You'll find no bottle juggling, just serious mixology, very dry martinis and, if you're lucky, a seat. Open until 3am.

6 U Tří Růží

MAP L5 ▪ Husova 10 ▪ 601 588281 ▪ www.u3r.cz

This very good Czech restaurant and microbrewery feels just right for the middle of Old Town. Beers brewed on the premises include a standard light, a dark lager, a Vienna red – from caramelized malt – and a wheat beer. The downstairs area can be crowded and noisy. Reservations are usually necessary to get a table.

Grand Café Orient's interior

7 Grand Café Orient

MAP N4 ▪ Ovocný trh 19 ▪ 224 224240 ▪ www.grandcafeorient.cz

This café was designed during the Cubist movement in 1912 by Josef Gočár. Patrons will love the building's architecture and be fascinated by the tower of cakes that greets them at the entrance. Grand Café Orient serves tea, breakfast and lunch menus, as well as wine and cocktails.

The traditional Hemingway Bar

8 Hemingway Bar

MAP J5 ▪ Karolíny Světlé 26 ▪ 773 974764 ▪ www.hemingwaybar.cz

This is an old-fashioned cocktail bar exactly as it should be, with formally dressed barmen polishing up the glassware before they pour you the perfect Old Fashioned or Whiskey Sour. The cocktail menu has hundreds of classic mixes, and even a selection of premium Czech, French and Swiss absinth. Book ahead or you're likely to be turned away.

9 Black Angel's

MAP L4 ▪ Staroměstské náměstí 29 ▪ 224 213807 ▪ www.blackangelsbar.cz

This bar, located in the second basement of hotel U Prince, boasts 1930s-style decor. In 2012, it was listed as one of the top 50 bars of the world by *The Sunday Times*. Sip on the excellent cocktails while enjoying fabulous views of the Old Town Square and City Centre.

10 Chapeau Rouge

MAP N3 ▪ Jakubská 2 ▪ 222 316328 ▪ www.chapeaurouge.cz

This bar next to the Basilica of St James (see p86) has lost some, but not all, of the seediness that characterized its previous incarnation, where the motto was "the customer is always wrong". Backpackers still chat each other up over absinth, however, and men in the street will offer you hashish on your way in. It may sound unappealing to some, but it is a true Prague experience.

Shops and Markets

1 Botanicus

Here you'll find oils and salts for that hot bath your travel-weary feet crave, as well as perfumes, candles, soaps and every natural health and beauty product you can imagine. Branches are scattered around town but the main one is off the Old Town Square *(see p88)*.

2 Artěl

MAP N4 ■ Celetná 29 (entrance from Rybná)

Named after a group of Bohemian artisans established in the early 1900s, Artěl has taken the time-honoured art of glassmaking and, working hand in hand with highly skilled craftspeople, has created a collection of fresh, whimsical yet elegant designs.

The chic interiors of Artěl

Decanters, Erpet Bohemia Crystal

3 Erpet Bohemia Crystal

MAP L4 ■ Staroměstské náměstí 27

A one-stop shop for glass and jewellery. Erpet sells Bohemian lead crystal, garnet jewellery, enamel glass and chandeliers, as well as fine goods from the Moser, Goebel and Swarovski manufacturers. Shoppers can ponder the purchases they're about to make over coffee in the shop's comfortable lounge area.

4 Art Deco

MAP L4 ■ Michalská 21

Enter this shop filled with antique furnishings, vintage clothing and one-of-a-kind knick-knacks and you'll feel you've stepped back into the First Republic. Kit yourself out in Jazz Age style, right down to the spats and cigarette holder, or dress up your parlour with an Art Nouveau clock or cordial set.

5 Dorotheum

MAP M4 ■ Ovocný trh 2

Dorotheum offices throughout the world trace their roots back to the Vienna pawnbroking office, established by Emperor Josef I in 1707. As a registered member of the Association of International Auctioneers, Dorotheum holds large auctions several times a year and maintains a

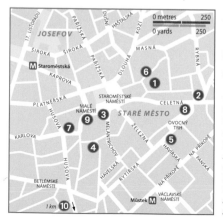

huge sales gallery of paintings and works of art, jewellery, silverware, glassware, fine china and furniture, as well as other collectors' items.

⑥ Cat's Gallery (Kočičí galerie)

MAP M3 ■ Staroměstské náměstí 20

This delightful little shop in Týnská street has vast collections of mugs, magnets, pictures, paintings, sculptures and other items that all have one thing in common – they depict cats in one form or another. This is a must-see for cat lovers and a great place to buy cat motif souvenirs, mementos and presents.

Cat's Gallery (Kočičí galerie)

⑦ Local Artists Praha

MAP L4 ■ Karlova 21

While walking through the "souvenir" Karlova street, set aside the time to stop at this small shop, where every item on display is a testimony to Czech traditional arts and crafts.

⑧ Hračky U zlatého lva

MAP N4 ■ Celetná 32

This centrally-located, multi-storey toyshop stocks a huge selection of traditional Czech wooden toys, most of them locally produced. There's a Krtek (Little Mole – the most popular Czech cartoon character) theme throughout which will please travelling tots in search of souvenirs.

⑨ Blue

Forget the traditional image of dust-collecting glass bowls and stemware. Blue's bold and quirky designs will light up your home like no old-fashioned glass can. Plus, the prices are low enough that you won't hesitate to use your purchases every day. You can also buy T-shirts and other gifts here *(see p88)*.

Vase, Blue

⑩ Náplavka Farmers' Market

MAP E6 ■ Náplavka ■ 8am–3pm Sat ■ www.farmarsketrziste.cz

This riverfront food market is the place to be on summer Saturdays when the whole city seems to turn out to buy fresh produce, breads and meats. Even if you're not shopping, the atmosphere is infectious. Stroll the embankment and have a beer or coffee at the pop-up cafés. Follow the Vltava south beyond the National Theatre to find the market *(see p59)*.

Náplavka Farmers' Market

🔟 Prague for Free

The medieval Astronomical Clock

1 Astronomical Clock
MAP L4 ■ Old Town Hall

Standing below the Gothic Old Town Hall, along with hundreds of fellow visitors, gawking up at the medieval clock as it goes through its hourly procession (on the hour from 9am to 11pm) is a rite of passage. It is rather brief and admittedly underwhelming, but a must-see (see p20).

2 Prague Castle Grounds
MAP C2 ■ Prague Castle
■ www.hrad.cz

Visiting the permanent collections at Prague Castle can cost a king's ransom in entry fees. What many visitors don't realize is that it is totally free to enter the castle grounds and wander around to your heart's content. Don't miss the changing of the castle guard on the hour from 7am to 8pm (till 6pm in winter).

3 Old Jewish Cemetery
Spread across seven sites in Prague, the Jewish Museum is world class, with impressive exhibits and admission fees priced to match. If paying the full fee is beyond your budget, you can catch a small but worthwhile glimpse of the multitude of sombre tombstones in the Old Jewish Cemetery for free through a small window set in the western wall of the cemetery on Ulice 17. listopadu (see p28–9).

4 John Lennon Wall
MAP D3 ■ Velkopřevorské náměstí, Malá Strana

This towering stretch of wall is covered with graffiti dedicated to Beatles frontman John Lennon. It is a relaxing – even spiritual – spot (see p93). Occasionally, buskers belt out their own renditions of "Yesterday" or "Imagine". Peaceful Kampa Island, a minute's walk to the east of the wall, is filled with hidden delights and well worth a wander (see p94).

5 Vyšehrad Cemetery
MAP B6 ■ Vyšehrad
■ www.praha-vysehrad.cz

The cemetery at Vyšehrad fortress is the country's most prominent burial ground and is free to enter. Fans of classical music will enjoy looking for the graves of Antonín Dvořák and Bedřich Smetana, among others. Many of the tombstones are works of art in their own right (see p123).

The grave of Antonín Dvořák

6 Feed the Swans
MAP D2 ■ Malá Strana

Feeding the swans on the Vltava is a great activity for kids – although you'll have to shell out for for seed mix (not bread as it makes the swans ill). The classic spot is on the Malá Strana side, south of the Malostranská metro station.

Swans on the Vltava

7 Free Walking Tours
MAP P4 ■ Old Town

■ www.extravaganzafreetour.com

This is a great way to explore Prague with a guide. Free Prague Tours is run by licensed English-speaking guides who are also history buffs and people-orientated. Even with a generous tip at the end, you'll still save money. Tours normally begin at the Powder Gate at 11am and 3:30pm.

8 View from Letná
MAP E1 ■ Greater Prague

Climb the steps at the northern end of Čechův most ("bridge" in Czech), north of Old Town Square for picture-postcard views of the Old Town and the bridges traversing the river below. Keep an eye out for the metronome on the hill *(see p124)*.

The Vltava, as seen from Letná

9 Wallenstein Garden
MAP D2 ■ Malá Strana ■ Open Apr–Oct: 7:30am–6pm Mon–Fri (from 10am weekends; to 7pm Jun–Sep)

■ www.senat.cz

Malá Strana is full of Renaissance and Baroque gardens that levy a fee to enter but this lovely 17th-century garden is free to the public *(see p52)*. The palace, home to the Czech Senate, can also be visited *(see p96)*.

10 Náplavka
MAP E6 ■ New Town

The embankment on the riverfront south of the National Theatre is home to nightly free summer con-certs, and a fun, popular farmers' market on Saturday mornings from April to October *(see p77)*.

TOP 10 MONEY-SAVING TIPS

A classical music performance

1 Opera and classical music in Prague is subsidized and tickets seldom cost more than a few hundred crowns.

2 Seek out pubs in outlying districts like the working-class Žižkov, where a half-litre (pint) mug of beer can cost half the price it does in the centre.

3 Even if you're not a fan of multibunk hostels, consider renting a private single or double hostel room. Many hostels offer these at a fraction of the price they would cost in a hotel.

4 Buy a discounted 1-day or 3-day pass for Prague's public transport. These are valid for the metro, trams, buses, trains and boats, as well as transfers between them throughout the city. You'll save money and be spared the inconvenience of buying individual tickets for each journey.

5 Eat out at lunchtime instead of dinner to take advantage of the popular three-course set menus.

6 Skip wine at meals in favour of beer. Czech wines can vary greatly in quality, the local beer is generally cheaper and excellent quality.

7 Resist the temptation to hop into a taxi. Most distances in the city are easily walkable, and public transport is reliable and cheap.

8 Consider renting an apartment rather than a hotel if you're staying for three days or longer. You'll not only save money but will have more privacy.

9 Time your stay to avoid the peak seasons around the Christmas, New Year and Easter holidays, when hotel rates go through the roof.

10 When arriving by plane, take the municipal bus into town from the airport. A single 32Kč ticket can often get you very close to your hotel.

TOP10 Festivals

A performance at the Prague Spring International Music Festival

1 Prague Spring International Music Festival
May–Jun

Bedřich Smetana's *Má vlast*, or *My Homeland (see p45)*, kicks off the annual three-week festival that draws classical music performers and fans from around the globe. The round of concerts closes with Beethoven's Ninth Symphony.

2 Bohemia International Folklore Dance Festival
Aug

This festival has been a success since its first staging in 2005. It has now expanded beyond Prague, as DanceBohemia, and brings amateur folklore dance ensembles together from all around the world.

3 May Day
1 May

It is customary for couples to visit the statue of the Czech Romantic poet Karel Hynek Mácha on Petřín Hill *(see pp38–9)*. For others the national holiday is spent trying to forget the old obligatory Communist rallies.

4 Karlovy Vary International Film Festival
Jul

It's easier to hobnob with the stars here than at Cannes or Berlin. Hundreds of partygoers turn the sleepy west Bohemian spa town, 130 km (81 miles) from Prague, upside down for nine days. Hundreds of screenings, too.

Performers at the Karlovy Vary

5 Prague Writer's Festival
Time varies every year

Salman Rushdie, Susan Sontag and Elie Wiesel are just some of the internationally acclaimed authors who have attended this annual event. The organizers often get grief for giving Czech writers short shrift.

6 Street Theatre Festival
Jul

Za dveřmi (Behind the Door) is an international street art festival that presents drama, acrobatics, parades and juggling on the streets and squares of Prague.

7 Tanec Praha
May, Jun

This international dance festival is on the verge of becoming something great. The local dance scene has greatly benefited from it, and audiences can now see contemporary productions all year round.

A race at the Pardubice Steeplechase

8 Pardubice Steeplechase
Oct

The first steeplechase here was held in 1874. With 31 jumps stretching over 7 km (4 miles), this is one of the biggest in Europe.

9 Masopust
Shrove Tue

Czech swine start getting nervous in early February as the nation whets its appetite and knives for their version of Carnival. While the beer-and-pork orgies are more common in villages, working-class Žižkov *(see p124)* throws a large party each year.

10 Mikuláš, Vánoce, Silvestr
Dec

Christmas celebrations are largely devoid of religion, but the mulled wine starts flowing on St Nicholas's Day and doesn't stop until the Christmas carp is all eaten and the New Year's Eve *(Silvestr)* fireworks arsenals are depleted.

TOP 10 NATIONAL HOLIDAYS

Traditional Czech Easter eggs

1 Renewal of the Independent Czech State
1 Jan
Marks the 1993 split of Czechoslovakia.

2 Easter Monday
Mar–Apr
Custom dictates that men give women a gentle whipping with a willow switch, and women respond with painted eggs.

3 Labour Day
1 May
Romantics lay flowers before the statue of Karel Hynek Mácha on Petřín Hill.

4 Day of Liberation
8 May
Plaques around town are adorned with flowers to remember those killed by the Germans in 1945.

5 Cyril and Methodius Day
5 Jul
The Greek missionaries brought both Christianity and the Cyrillic alphabet to the Slavs *(see p49)*.

6 Jan Hus Day
6 Jul
Czechs head for the hills where they roast sausages *(see p43)*.

7 Czech Statehood Day
28 Sep
Bohemia's history is recalled on St Wenceslas Day, as most Czechs call it.

8 Independence Day
28 Oct
In 1918 Czechoslovakia declared itself independent of Austro-Hungary.

9 Day of the Fight for Freedom and Democracy
17 Nov
The Velvet Revolution anniversary is marked with candles and flowers.

10 Christmas
24–26 Dec
Streets fill with carp sellers and hedonists drinking mulled wine.

Prague
Area by Area

The Vltava flowing through
Prague's historical core

Old Town	**84**
Malá Strana	**92**
Prague Castle and Hradčany	**100**
Josefov	**108**
New Town	**114**
Greater Prague	**122**

TOP 10 Old Town

Prague's heart is a layered cake of history: the oldest of its buildings have double cellars, owing to a flood-prevention programme that buried the original streets 3 m (10 ft) beneath those that exist today. Architecturally, it embraces every epoch, from the Romanesque to the Brutalist style of the mid-1970s Kotva department store. Historically, the burghers of the Old Town (Staré Město) were ill at ease with the castle district, and vice versa, with the town being a bastion of Protestant feistiness. The Old Town is still livelier than Malá Strana and Hradčany, with cafés, clubs, restaurants and theatres that keep it buzzing around the clock.

Municipal House

OLD TOWN

Old Town Square

1 Old Town Square

Over the centuries, this now peaceful square at the heart of the city has witnessed hundreds of executions, political capitulations and, more recently of course, riotous ice-hockey celebrations, a sport about which the Czechs are fanatical. Today, the action is more likely to come from the crowds of tourists and Praguers, enjoying a coffee or a mug of beer at one of the numerous pavement cafés. Dominated by the splendid Church of Our Lady before Týn, the square is always buzzing; in winter and summer, it's a wonderful place to watch the world go by (see pp18–21).

2 Municipal House
MAP P3 ▪ Náměstí Republiky 5
▪ 222 002101 for tours ▪ Adm ▪ www.obecnidum.cz

National Revival artist Alfons Mucha was one of many to lend his talents to the Municipal House (Obecní dům), Prague's star Art Nouveau attraction. One of its most beautiful and striking features is Karel Špillar's mosaic above the main entrance, entitled *Homage to Prague*. It also has a firm place in history as it was from the Municipal House that Czechoslovakia was declared an independent state in 1918. Today, it is home to restaurants, cafés, exhibition halls, shops and the Prague Symphony Orchestra at the Smetana Hall (see p66).

3 Powder Gate
MAP P4 ▪ Náměstí Republiky
▪ Open Apr–Sep: 10am–10pm; Oct, Mar: 10am–8pm; Nov–Feb: 10am–6pm ▪ Adm
▪ en.muzeumprahy.cz

In the 15th century, King Vladislav II laid the cornerstone for this tower at the city's eastern gate, intended to complement the Royal Court nearby. Its name comes from its 17th-century role as a gunpowder store. The tower was damaged during Prussian attacks in 1757. The Neo-Gothic façade seen today, with its sculptural decoration, dates from 1876.

Powder Gate

① **Top 10 Sights**
see pp85–7

① **Restaurants**
see p91

① **Cafés and Pubs**
see p90

① **Shops**
see p88

① **Nightclubs**
see p89

4 Celetná
MAP M4

The medieval route from the silver-mining town of Kutná Hora in Bohemia passed down the street known today as Celetná, through Old Town Square and on to Prague Castle. There is still a lot of traffic on the gently curving street today.

Traditional house sign, Celetná

5 Basilica of St James
MAP N3 ▪ Malá Štupartská 6 ▪ Open 9:30am–noon & 2–4pm daily (except Mon & during Mass) ▪ praha. minorite.cz

The Gothic and Baroque interior wins the award for Prague's creepiest sanctuary. The church, founded in 1232 by Wenceslas I, is best known for the legend of the mummified arm hanging above the door (see p60), but don't miss one of the organ recitals held here (see p67).

6 Clementinum
MAP K4 ▪ Křížovnická 190, Mariánské náměstí 5 & Karlova 1 ▪ 733 129252 ▪ Open 10am–4:30pm daily (to 6pm Mar–Oct; to 5:30pm Nov–Dec); concerts from 6pm daily (from 5pm Nov–May) ▪ Adm ▪ www.klementinum.com

Built in the mid-17th century as a Jesuit college, the Clementinum now houses the National Library. Astronomer Johannes Kepler (see p43) discovered the laws of planetary motion atop the Astronomical Tower. There is a beautiful Baroque library, and the Mirror Chapel hosts various concerts.

7 Ungelt
MAP M3

Also known as the Týn Courtyard, this was a fortified merchants settlement in the 10th century. The Baroque and Renaissance houses were completely renovated in the early 1990s, creating what is now one of the Old Town's most charming mercantile centres.

Buildings within the Ungelt complex

8 Karlova
MAP K4

You will inevitably get lost trying to follow Karlova street from the Old Town Square to Charles Bridge; relax and enjoy the bewildering, twisting alleys crammed with shops and cafés.

Clementinum

St Nicholas's Church, Old Town

(9) St Nicholas's Church

MAP L3 ▪ Staroměstské náměstí ▪ Open 10am–4pm daily ▪ Adm for Masses and concerts ▪ www.svmikulas.cz

This Baroque jewel started life as a parish church. During World War II, it was used as a garrison for Czech troops. It now belongs to the Hussite Church and also operates as a concert hall (see p18).

(10) Bethlehem Square

MAP K5 ▪ Chapel: Open 10am–6pm daily (to 6:30pm Apr–Oct) ▪ Adm ▪ www.bethlehemchapel.eu

The 15th-century Catholic reformer Jan Hus (see p19) preached in the reconstructed chapel on the square's north side. The church was converted into apartments in the 18th century but was lovingly restored to its former state in the 1950s.

PRAGUE'S WALLS AND GATES

Prague's walls started going up in the 13th century, protecting the new settlement from the distant Tartars. The town was accessible via wall gates. As gradual developments in military technology made walls and moats less effective forms of defence, Praguers found new uses for their fortifications. The broad ramparts became parks, complete with benches, lamps and even cafés. Prague kept the habit of locking its gates at night well into the 19th century, however.

Powder Gate detail

A STROLL AROUND THE OLD TOWN

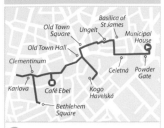

▶ MORNING

After breakfast at the **Municipal House** café (see p85), take a guided tour of the building, then go and climb the **Powder Gate** (see p85) next door for the views before the caffeine wears off.

Wander down **Celetná**, ducking through the arcade to Štupartská and the **Basilica of St James**. If you have at least 45 minutes before the top of the hour, make your way through the **Ungelt** courtyard to the **Old Town Square** (see p85). Join a tour of the **Old Town Hall** and get a backstage view of the Apostles' show on the Astronomical Clock (see pp20–21). Otherwise, spend some time shopping in the Ungelt, then join the crowd below the clock outside to see the spectacle.

For lunch, head south out of the square to **Kogo Havelská** (see p91) for delicious contemporary food.

AFTERNOON

Return to the Old Town Square and do a quick circumnavigation, then enter the meandering turns of **Karlova** and wander leisurely past the area's old buildings before turning south to reach **Bethlehem Square**. Take a tour of the lovely Bethlehem Chapel, then retrace your steps to Karlova to visit the **Clementinum**.

If you'd like a little break, have coffee and cake at the excellent **Café Ebel** (see p90), a two-minute walk south, before freshening up and taking in a concert or a performance at the theatre. Curtains go up around 7:30pm, so it is sensible to dine afterwards.

See map on pp84–5

Shops

① Blue
MAP L4 ▪ Malé náměstí 14

A dazzlingly different kind of glass shop stocking modern, fun and quirky designs in bowls, knick-knacks, t-shirts and other tourist fare (see p77).

Glass being blown at Moser

② Moser
MAP M4 ▪ Staroměstké nám. 15

Classic crystal and cut-glass objects produced by this well-known manufacturer. Even if you're not interested in a large vase or a crystal hedgehog, it's worth a look around.

③ Charles University Gift Shop
MAP M4 ▪ Celetná 14

Looking for cool souvenirs to take back for the kids? Problem solved: get them a Charles University pullover. If it's chilly outdoors, you'll probably want to get one for yourself as well.

④ Franz Kafka Bookshop
MAP M3 ▪ Staroměstské náměstí 12

Here you can find a wide range of Czech literature in translation, coffee-table books and catalogues from recent exhibitions held next door at the Municipal Gallery, alongside classical music CDs.

⑤ Material
MAP M3 ▪ Týn 1, Ungelt

Czech tradition in designer crystal and glassware gets a modern makeover at this shop in the Ungelt courtyard, not far from the Old Town Square. Admire the eye-catching stemware, vases, dishes and candle-holders, all presented in a space that fuses classical and modern design.

⑥ Botanicus
MAP M3 ▪ Týn 3

The store's all-natural health and beauty products are produced at a "historic village" east of Prague; enquire about tours. Sells herbs, oils and other seasonings, too (see p76).

⑦ Manufaktura
MAP L4 ▪ Melantrichova 17

One-stop shopping for your small souvenir needs, including Czech folk crafts and traditional wooden toys. In addition to these items, there are also naturally made cosmetics and toiletries featuring an odd assortment of ingredients, like Czech beer, wine and thermal salt.

⑧ Czech Folk Crafts
MAP K4 ▪ Karlova 26

Kids these days might not appreciate the handmade wooden toys or corn-husk dolls, but when was the last time you bought yourself a gift?

⑨ Český Porcelán
MAP M5 ▪ Perlová 1

Bohemian porcelain might not be as prestigious as Bohemian crystal, but it makes a pretty souvenir or present.

Porcelain jug at Český Porcelán

⑩ Keramika
MAP M5 ▪ Havelská 21

Probably every Czech kitchen has at least one of these ceramic plates. The traditional Czech folk patterns are blue, red or yellow.

Nightclubs

1 Double Trouble
MAP L4 ■ Melantrichova 17

Billed as Prague's most popular Gothic cellar nightclub, Double Trouble offers an electrifying atmosphere. DJs play dance music every night, and people dancing on tables or seats is the norm.

2 Karlovy lázně

Weekends draw a queue of young clubbers stretching along the riverbank waiting to get in to these remodelled municipal baths. Four levels of clubbing, from classic rock to DJs and, occasionally, live bands (see p69). Bruce Willis jammed here when in town.

3 Roxy

The Old Town's most exciting club. In addition to the best dance parties in town, the former cinema hosts experimental theatre, live bands and art exhibitions (see p68).

4 Coyotes
MAP L4 ■ Malé náměstí 2

The dance floor is not the biggest in the city, but Coyotes has a spectacular light show that puts other, bigger clubs in Prague to shame.

5 Vagon
MAP L6 ■ Národní třída 25

One of the originals for exciting live music, this place hosts blues or rock bands most nights, with a mix of well-known and unsigned acts. Always a lively atmosphere.

The bar area at Vagon

The AghaRTA Jazz Centrum club

6 AghaRTA Jazz Centrum
MAP M4 ■ Železná 16

Named after Miles Davis's seminal album from the 1970s and opened the day after his death, this club has daily performances by top Czech musicians and hosts the annual AghaRTA Prague Jazz Festival.

7 Klub Lávka
MAP J5 ■ Novotného lávka 1

Atmospherically located right by Charles Bridge, this discobar is open 24 hours a day. In summer, you can enjoy the terrace and garden restaurant, and even rent a boat.

8 Friends
MAP K6 ■ Bartolomějská 11

The name fits. Prague's best gay cocktail bar has a steady following among expat and local men who are less interested in cruising than in just having a drink with like-minded folks. The owner Michael will tell you what's what.

9 Zlatý Strom
MAP K4 ■ Karlova 6

Enjoy unusual views of the Prague night sky through the glass ceilings of this subterranean club. There are two dance floors and an aquarium.

10 Limonádový Joe
MAP P1 ■ Revoluční 1

This laid-back and fun club, under the Kotva department store, hosts everything from nineties nights to fashion shows and retro Czechoslovak hit discos. It generally attacts a mixed, slightly older crowd.

See map on pp84–5

Cafés and Pubs

1 Café Obecní dům
MAP P3 ▪ Náměstí Republiky 5

Dressed to the nines in Art Nouveau splendour, the café at the Municipal House glitters. Stop in for breakfast before setting off for a day exploring the Old Town and its sights.

2 Café de Paris
MAP P3 ▪ Hotel Paříž, U Obecního domu 1

If you're not already staying at the Hotel Paříž, you may be tempted to take a room just so you can have your morning coffee in this lovely Jugendstil café. Superior service.

3 Lokál
MAP N2 ▪ Dlouhá 33
▪ 222 316265 ▪

Rumoured to serve the city's freshest Pilsner Urquell beer, delivered to the door in big tanks. They also serve better-than-average traditional Czech pub meals – think goulash and roast pork – at very reasonable prices. Advance booking is essential.

4 Café Ebel
MAP L5 ▪ Řetezová 9

You won't find a better cup of coffee in the city than at Ebel, which uses beans from all over the world. Not far from the Old Town Square.

5 Týnská Literární kavárna
MAP M3 ▪ Týnská 6

Local customers here are serious about their literature at this café attached to a bookstore. The hidden courtyard is a blissfully quiet space to enjoy a beer on summer nights.

6 Grand Café Praha
MAP M4 ▪ Staroměstské náměstí 22

Unlike other establishments on the square, this coffee house actually offers great value and good service.

7 La Bottega di Finestra
MAP K4 ▪ Platnéřská 11
▪ 222 233094

This café caters for all tastes, with a range of Italian specialities that includes pasta dishes and vegetarian options. Breakfast is also served.

8 Prague Beer Museum
MAP N2 ▪ Dlouhá 46
▪ 732 330912

This "museum" is actually a popular pub with around 30 Czech beers on tap.

9 Atmoška
MAP J5 ▪ Smetanovo náb. 14

This café, pub and restaurant offers its customers ultimate views of Prague Castle rising up on Hradčany across the Vltava and of the cobblestoned Charles Bridge nearby.

10 Hotel U Prince
MAP L4
▪ Staroměstské náměstí 29 ▪ 737 261842

Treat yourself to an unforgettable dining experience on the lovely rooftop terrace of Hotel U Prince. The eatery serves as both a café and a restaurant.

Rooftop, Hotel U Prince

Restaurants

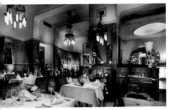

Elegant interior of Sarah Bernhardt

PRICE CATEGORIES

For a three-course meal for one with half a bottle of wine (or equivalent meal), taxes and extra charges.

(Kč) under Kč500 (Kč)(Kč) Kč500–Kč1,000
(Kč)(Kč)(Kč) over Kč1,000

1 Sarah Bernhardt

MAP P3 ■ Hotel Paříž, U Obecního domu 1 ■ 222 195877 ■ (Kč)(Kč)(Kč)

French cuisine in an opulent Art Nouveau setting inspired by Alfons Mucha's paintings of the French actress. Bohumil Hrabal *(see p45)* celebrated the hotel in his novel *I Served the King of England*.

2 Café Imperial

MAP G2 ■ Na Poříčí 15 ■ (Kč)(Kč)

A busy and popular eatery. Enjoy a seven-course menu with selected wines at the Chef's Table, set up in the middle of the bustling kitchen.

3 Pasta Fresca

MAP M4 ■ Celetná 11 ■ 224 230244 ■ (Kč)(Kč)(Kč)

Chef Tomáš Mykytyn makes regional Italian dishes using fresh seasonal ingredients. Sommeliers are on hand to guide diners through the vast wine selection.

4 Kogo Havelská

MAP M4 ■ Havelská 27 ■ 224 214543 ■ (Kč)(Kč)(Kč)

Serving superior Italian dishes at remarkably low prices, Kogo Havelská is popular with discerning locals; book ahead. Marvellous service.

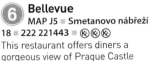

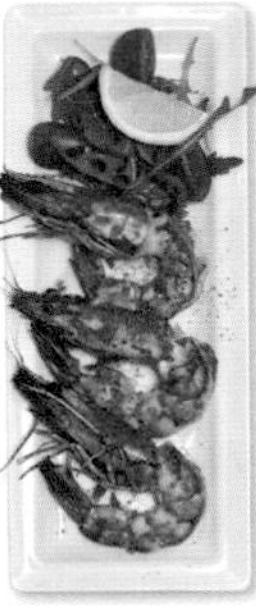

King prawns at Kogo Havelská

5 Divinis

MAP M3 ■ Týnská 21 ■ 222 325440 ■ (Kč)(Kč)(Kč)

This high-end wine bar and restaurant manages to balance a modern feel with a traditional Italian atmosphere. Good-quality wines complement the classic Sicilian specialities.

6 Bellevue

MAP J5 ■ Smetanovo nábřeží 18 ■ 222 221443 ■ (Kč)(Kč)(Kč)

This restaurant offers diners a gorgeous view of Prague Castle rising above Charles Bridge, and formal Continental dining.

7 Dutá Hlava

MAP L5 ■ Betlémské náměstí 5a ■ 602 250082 ■ (Kč)(Kč)

Situated in a medieval cellar, this casual club has a menu of international food and some very well-executed Czech staples.

8 Lehká Hlava

MAP K5 ■ Boršov 2 ■ 222 220665 ■ (Kč)

This vegetarian restaurant offers customers a varied menu which is so good you don't even notice there are no meat choices.

9 Modrý Zub Dlouhá Long Street Food

MAP N2 ■ Dlouhá 21 ■ 222 313 340 ■ (Kč)(Kč)

This modest restaurant offers classic Thai dishes of phad thai and beef rendang, alongside spicy Asian street food.

10 Staroměstská

MAP M4 ■ Staroměstské náměstí 19 ■ 224 213015 ■ (Kč)(Kč)

Classic Czech dishes and a wide selection of beers are served at this traditional inn.

See map on pp84–5

📰10 Malá Strana

Malá Strana, now known as the "Little Quarter", was originally called the New Town, long before Charles IV moved that name across the river *(see pp114–21)*. Floods, fires and war kept construction going on the Vltava's left bank; very few of the original Romanesque and Gothic buildings remain. During the reign of the Habsburgs, grand palaces were built in Baroque style, and today many of these serve as parliament or government buildings and embassies. The area is an enclave of parks, cafés, winding streets and unassuming churches.

Malá Strana tower, Charles Bridge

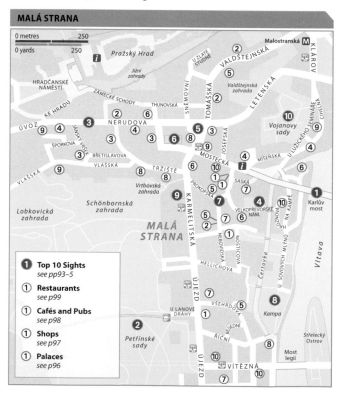

MALÁ STRANA

- **1** Top 10 Sights
  see pp93–5
- **①** Restaurants
  see p99
- **①** Cafés and Pubs
  see p98
- **①** Shops
  see p97
- **①** Palaces
  see p96

A view of the Vltava and Charles Bridge, as seen from Petřín Hill

1 Charles Bridge

For almost all visitors to Prague, this spectacular Gothic bridge, crossing the Vltava from the Old Town to the castle complex, remains their most memorable image of the city long after they have returned home (see pp22–3).

2 Petřín Hill

A more than welcome respite from the tiny, generally crowded streets in the city below is this sprawling park looking down over spires and rooftops. Enjoy the views all the way up the hill by taking the funicular (see pp38–9).

The Golden Horseshoe, Nerudova 34

3 Nerudova
MAP C2

The 19th-century Czech writer and poet Jan Neruda (1834–91) lived in the House of the Two Suns, at the top of the street that now bears his name. Lined with former palaces, Nerudova street leads uphill from Malostranské náměstí, its many winding side streets leading visitors up to Prague Castle (see pp12–15).

Traditionally an artists' quarter, the street is worth exploring for its many craft shops and galleries. It is also home to one of the most concentrated collections of historic house signs in the city (see pp54–5).

4 John Lennon Wall
MAP D3 ■ Velkopřevorské náměstí

Prague hippies and the secret police once waged a long-running paint battle here, as the latter constantly tried to eradicate the graffiti artists' work. The original artwork, created by students after Lennon's assassination, has been painted over many times (see p61), but the John Lennon Peace Club still gathers annually at this self-made shrine to sing the former Beatle's praises – and his songs.

Artwork on the John Lennon Wall

Trams at Malostranské náměstí

THE HEDONISTS' QUARTER

The district of Malá Strana became something of a party town for the Viennese nobility during the 18th century. Wolfgang Amadeus Mozart strayed from the straight and narrow here, as did Casanova – in his sunset years, the ageing playboy penned his memoirs at the palace that is now home to the British Embassy. The trend continues today, with Prague's youth gathering in the little squares to play music, smoke and drink.

5 Malostranské náměstí
MAP C2

The hectic traffic that now detracts from the beauty of Malá Strana's main square seems historically fitting – in the past it has been witness to innumerable destructive fires, revolutions and executions (during the days when a gallows stood here). St Nicholas's Church and the adjoining Jesuit college dominate the centre of the square, while lovely Neo-Classical palace arcades and restaurants line the perimeter. One of the most important buildings is the Sněmovna, home to the lower house of the Czech parliament, the Chamber of Deputies.

6 St Nicholas's Church
MAP C2 ▪ Malostranské náměstí ▪ Open Mar–Oct: 9am–5pm daily; Nov–Feb: 9am–4pm daily ▪ Adm ▪ www.stnicholas.cz

Jesuits constructed this stunning example of Baroque architecture in the early 18th century. This prominent Prague landmark was designed by the acclaimed father and son Baroque architects, Christoph and Kilian Dientzenhofer, while other leading artists adorned the interior with exquisite carvings, statues and frescoes. From the 1950s the clock tower often served as an observation and spying point for the state security (Communist police).

7 Maltézské náměstí
MAP C3

The Knights of Malta once had an autonomous settlement here, and the square still bears their name. The area is dominated by beautiful Baroque palaces, and the 12th-century Church of Our Lady below the Chain, whose name refers to the chain used in the Middle Ages to close the monastery gatehouse.

8 Kampa Island
MAP D3–4

The tiny Čertovka (Devil's Canal) that separates Kampa from Malá Strana was once the town's "laundry", milling area and, in the 17th century, home to a thriving pottery industry. A popular park now covers the island's southern end (see p52), while the northern half is home to elegant embassies, restaurants and hotels. Much of the island was submerged during the 2002 flooding and many buildings had to be repaired.

Kampa Island and the Čertovka canal

Church of Our Lady Victorious

9 Church of Our Lady Victorious

MAP C3 ▪ Karmelitská 9 ▪ Open 8:30am–7pm Mon–Sat (to 8pm Sun) ▪ Museum of the Prague Infant Jesus: 9:30am–5:30pm Mon–Sat, 1–6pm Sun

Also known as the Church of the Infant Jesus of Prague, Prague's first Baroque church (1611) got its name – and its Catholic outlook – after the Battle of White Mountain (see p42). Visitors stream in to see the church's miracle-working statue of the Christ Child (see p48).

10 Vojanovy sady

MAP D2 ▪ U lužického semináře

Malá Strana has many green pockets, but Vojan's gardens top them all for their romantic charm. Tulip beds, flowering fruit trees and the occasional peacock add to the fairy-tale atmosphere (see p52).

A DAY IN MALÁ STRANA

▶ MORNING

You can approach the Little Quarter from the Old Town as royal processions once did, by crossing Charles Bridge (see p93), or you can save your energy for the day ahead, and start from the top of the hill and walk down. Get to **Nerudova** (see p93) from one of the many side streets leading from Hradčany and stroll down, window shopping at the many craft outlets on your way. Don't worry if you stray off the beaten path; as long as you go downhill, you'll end up at the area's central hub, **Malostranské náměstí**. Here, spend at least an hour savouring one of the city's most spectacular buildings, St Nicholas's Church. Pause for lunch at one of the many pleasant cafés on Malostranské náměstí.

AFTERNOON

After lunch, take Tomášská to the **Wallenstein Garden** (see p52). Tiptoe through the tulips at **Vojanovy sady** and continue down U lužického semináře, pausing for a cup of coffee at **Čertovka** (see p98). Continue under Charles Bridge and onto the lovely **Kampa Island**. Explore the island, then head off to check the writing on the **John Lennon Wall** (see p93) before visiting the **Church of Our Lady Victorious**.

In the evening, catch a recital at St Nicholas's Church, or head over to the **Blue Light Bar** (see p69) to carouse with what feels, on some nights, like half the city.

See map on p92 ←

Palaces

1 Nostitz Palace
MAP D3 ■ Maltézské náměstí 1

Take in the restoration work at this 17th-century palace while enjoying a chamber music concert. The palace now serves as the seat of the Czech Ministry of Culture.

2 Thun-Hohenstein Palace
MAP C2 ■ Nerudova 20

The Kolowrat family's heraldic eagles support the portal of this palace. Built by Giovanni Santini-Aichel in 1721, the building is now home to the Italian Embassy.

3 Liechtenstein Palace
MAP C2 ■ Malostranské náměstí 13 ■ www.amu.cz

Originally several different houses, the Liechtenstein Palace fused in the 16th century. Today, it is home to Prague's Academy of Music and numerous concerts and recitals.

4 Morzin Palace
MAP C2 ■ Nerudova 5

The two giant Moors (hence Morzin) bearing up the Romanian Embassy's façade are said to wander about Malá Strana streets at night.

Wallenstein Palace ceiling frescoes

5 Wallenstein Palace
MAP D2 ■ Valdštejnské náměstí 4 ■ Open 10am–5pm Sat & Sun ■ Adm ■ www.senat.cz

General Wallenstein pulled out all the stops creating what is essentially

Façade of the Nostitz Palace

a monument to himself. On the palace's frescoes, the Thirty Years' War commander had himself depicted as both Achilles and Mars.

6 Buquoy Palace
MAP D3 ■ Velkopřevorské náměstí 2

This pink stucco palace and the John Lennon Wall are separated by only a few steps, but they are miles apart aesthetically. The French Ambassador helped preserve the graffiti opposite his offices in the 1980s.

7 Michna Palace
MAP C4 ■ Újezd 40

Francesco Caratti modelled this palace on Versailles in the 17th century. It is home to the Sokol Physical Culture Movement.

8 Schoenborn Palace
MAP C3 ■ Tržiště 15

Count Colloredo-Mansfeld owned the palace in the 17th century: having lost a leg in the Thirty Years' War, he had the stairs rebuilt so he could ride his horse into the building. Czechoslovakia's first ambassador to the United States sold the palace to the US government in 1925.

9 Lobkowicz Palace (Převorovských)
MAP B3 ■ Vlašská 19

Home to the German Embassy. In 1989 hundreds of East Germans found their way to the West by scrambling over the back fence of this embassy building.

10 Kaunitz Palace
MAP C3 ■ Mostecká 15

The Yugoslav (now Serbian) Embassy sat quietly in its pink and yellow stucco palace for more than 300 years until war made it a popular spot for protests.

Shops

1 Beer Shop Galerie Piva
MAP D3 ▪ Lázeňská 15

A large variety of bottled beers from around the country, mostly from independent producers, are sold at this store. The knowledgeable staff will helpfully guide you through the offerings available.

2 V Ráji
MAP C2 ▪ Tomášská 10

This bookstore and publishing house specializes in foreign books on Prague. Dictionaries, calendars, postcards and other items in 21 languages are on offer.

3 Elima
MAP C3 ▪ Jánský vršek 5

Buried in the backstreets of Malá Strana, this small, attractive shop sells wonderful handmade Polish pottery from the Boleslawiec area for very reasonable prices.

4 Obchod vším možným
MAP B2 ▪ Nerudova 45

Just under New Castle Steps, at the end of Nerudova street, this small shop sells original Czech puppets, gifts, toys, ceramics, jewellery, art and enamel tableware.

Exterior of Obchod vším možným

5 Galeria Kotrba
MAP C3 ▪ Maltézské náměstí 3

Set right in the middle of Maltese Square is this small shop filled with lovely old paintings, maps and engravings of Prague. You may be surprised to see how the city has changed over time.

6 Decastello
MAP C3 ▪ Karmelitská 26

A delightful small shop offering a variety of products from jewellery and ceramics to home textiles and replicas of old weapons.

Květinářstvi u Červéneho lva

7 Květinářstvi u Červéneho lva
MAP D3 ▪ Saská

It appears as if a jungle is sprouting from the hole in the wall that is the Flowershop at the Red Lion. Spruce up your apartment or hotel room with their unique arrangements.

8 Malostranské starožitnictví
MAP C2 ▪ Malostranské náměstí 28

This antiques store is a veritable treasure trove of jewellery, watches, porcelain objects, silverware, coins and photographs. It also sells larger items, such as musical instruments.

9 Absinth Shop
MAP B2 ▪ Úvoz 1

Situated under the Castle Steps in a colourful Art Nouveau building, this shop offers an assortment of Czech absinth, as well as absinth from elsewhere in Europe. Tastings are free. *Slivovitz* (plum brandy), wines, *becherovka* liquor and special cannabis beers are also on sale.

10 Vetešnictví
MAP C4 ▪ Vítězná 16

A favourite junk shop, where you can find everything from silver teaspoons to glass and door handles.

See map on p92 ←

Cafés and Pubs

Snacks at Bohemia Bagel

1 Bohemia Bagel
MAP D3 ■ Lázeňská 19

It's hard to believe now, but Prague had no bagels until an American entrepreneur opened this shop here in 1997, serving fresh-baked bagels, sandwiches and endless cups of coffee. Open until 7pm. The same people run the jazz club U Malého Glena (see p69).

2 U Hada
MAP C3 ■ Maltézské náměstí 3

This tiny wine cellar sells excellent imported and domestic wines. If the tables out front are full, take your bottle to Petřín Hill.

3 Baráčnická rychta
MAP C3 ■ Tržiště 23

This wood-panelled beer hall, housed in a Modernist 1930s building, is a little piece of traditional Czech Republic in Malá Strana.

4 Restaurant and Beer Parlor Čertovka
MAP D2 ■ U lužického semináře 24

The stairway leading to this café's riverside patio is so narrow it needs its own traffic lights. They say President Václav Havel took Pink Floyd here for beer.

5 Bar Bar
MAP D4 ■ Všehrdova 17

The salads, burgers and crêpes served here make an excellent light lunch. This place is very popular in the evenings, so seats are hard to find.

6 U Kocoura
MAP C2 ■ Nerudova 2

You might think the regulars at this pub on Malá Strana's main drag would be used to tourists by now, but don't be surprised if every face turns to meet you. Serves excellent Pilsner.

7 Café Lounge
MAP C4 ■ Plaská 615/8

Admire the beautiful interiors and courtyard of this café. Every week there are different coffee and wine specials. Don't miss the superb, imaginative desserts.

8 Café Bella Vida
MAP D4 ■ Malostranské nábřezí 3

This café serves its own coffee blend as well as delectable mini-desserts and sandwiches.

9 Café Victoria
MAP C2 ■ Malostranské náměstí 38

Founded in 1881, this café offers tasty meals alfresco in its garden or inside where there is a permanent exhibition by photographer Jan Saudek.

Interior of the John Lennon Pub

10 John Lennon Pub
MAP D3 ■ Hroznová 6

This pub is all about celebrating the legendary singer. Enjoy steaks and burgers in the garden.

Restaurants

PRICE CATEGORIES
For a three-course meal for one with half a bottle of wine (or equivalent meal), taxes and extra charges.

Kč under Kč500 KčKč Kč500–Kč1,000
KčKčKč over Kč1,000

1 Cantina

MAP C4 ■ Újezd 38 ■ 257 317173 ■ KčKč

The best Mexican food in Prague. The fajitas are great; try the chicken and banana variety. Book ahead.

2 Pálffy Palác

MAP D2 ■ Valdštejnská 14 ■ 257 530522 ■ KčKčKč

This fine dining establishment with a great view of the castle terraces seems to revel in its somewhat shabby splendour *(see p71)*.

3 Malostranská Beseda

MAP C2 ■ Malostranské náměstí 21 ■ 257 409112 ■ KčKč

Set in an elegant building in the heart of Little Quarter, this cosy and buzzing place serves traditional Czech food and beer.

4 U Patrona

MAP D3 ■ Dražického náměstí 4 ■ 257 530725 ■ KčKč

The Continental and Czech cuisine will please gourmets; the balcony overlooking Charles Bridge will delight romantics.

5 El Centro

MAP C3 ■ Maltézské náměstí 9 ■ 257 533343 ■ KčKč

The Spanish owners and chefs ensure the *paella* is just right at this authentic and popular eatery.

6 Kampa Park

MAP D3 ■ Na Kampě 8b ■ 257 532685 ■ KčKčKč

This top riverside restaurant has three terraces and a winter garden. It serves a mix of Continental classics and fusion cuisine.

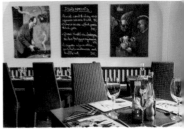

Tables at U malé velryby

7 U malé velryby

MAP C3 ■ Maltézské náměstí 15 ■ 257 214703 ■ KčKč

The "Little Whale" offers diners new twists on old classics in an affordable Czech brasserie style, with plenty of regularly changing options from calamari to steaks.

8 Gitanes

MAP C3 ■ Tržiště 7 ■ 257 530163 ■ KčKč

A short walk from Charles Bridge, this unpretentious restaurant serves the best of Dalmatian cuisine.

9 Malostranská pivnice

MAP D2 ■ Cihelná 3 ■ 257 530032 ■ KčKč

Old pub-style restaurant with traditional Czech fare and excellent Pilsner beer.

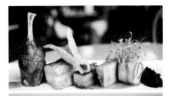

Appetizers at Café Savoy

10 Café Savoy

MAP C4 ■ Vítězná 5 ■ 257 311562 ■ KčKčKč

This feels just like a Prague café should, with high ceilings, elegant fixtures and huge windows. It has a standard as well as gourmet menu.

See map on p92 ←

TOP 10 Prague Castle and Hradčany

Founded by Prince Bořivoj in the 9th century, Prague Castle and its attendant cathedral tower overlook the city from the long hill known as Hradčany. The surrounding town was founded in 1320, becoming home to servants' hovels and, after the cataclysmic fire of 1541, grand palaces. Renaissance and Baroque reconstructions in the area created much of what visitors see today. The Loreto shrine to the Virgin Mary demonstrated the growing importance of Prague to the church. At the castle, primitive defences were removed, making room for gardens, parade grounds and the other needs of a modern empire. When the Habsburgs removed the imperial seat to Vienna, Hradčany seemed to become preserved in time, saving it from the ravages of war and modernization. The area abounds with interesting sights for art and history lovers, as well as romantic hidden lanes and parks – in short, a total expression of the Czech nation's shifting epochs and politics.

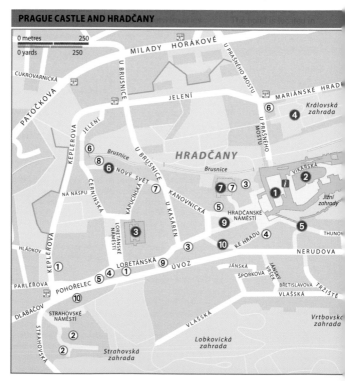

PRAGUE CASTLE AND HRADČANY

Prague Castle rising above the town

1 Prague Castle

The first and main focus of most tourists' visit to the city of Prague is the majestically located and architecturally varied castle complex (see pp12–15). Its determined survival in the face of an often turbulent history seems only to heighten the castle's lure for tourists. Despite its medieval appearance, it is still as much of a political stronghold as it has always been, and currently serves as the office of the country's president, Miloš Zeman.

2 St Vitus Cathedral

The Gothic splendour of St Vitus's spires can be seen from almost every vantage point in the city, but don't miss the opportunity to see its beautiful stained-glass windows and gargoyles up close (see pp16–17).

3 The Loreto

The onion-domed white towers of this Baroque 17th-century church complex are like something out of a fairy tale (see pp26–7).

4 Royal Garden

MAP C1 ■ U Prašného mostu ■ Open Apr–Oct: 10am–6pm daily (to 7pm May & Sep; to 8pm Aug; to 9pm Jun & Jul) ■ www.hrad.cz

This garden was originally laid out in 1534 by Ferdinand I. Although today's visitors may regret the disappearance of the maze and the pineapple trees that once featured here, they are likely to appreciate the absence of Rudolf II's freely roaming lions and tigers. In the English-style garden are the former presidential residence (the First Lady didn't like it), the sgraffitoed Ball Game Hall and the Royal Summer Palace, also known as the Belvedere.

Flowerbeds at the Royal Garden

5 New Castle Steps
MAP C2

The Royal Route, established in the 15th century for the coronation of George of Poděbrady, covered the distance from the Municipal House on the Náměstí Republiky (see p85) to the castle. The last stretch climbed the hill here at the Zámecké schody, although the original steps were reconstructed during Empress Maria Theresa's Hradčany renovation in the 18th century. Halfway up is a music pavilion, from which a brass quartet of the Castle Guard serenades the city each morning at 10am.

6 Nový Svět
MAP A2

Nestled below The Loreto (see pp26–7), at the head of the Stag Moat, is Nový Svět (New World), the best street in town for a romantic stroll. The picturesque low houses were built in the 17th century to replace slums built for castle workers after their houses burned down in 1541. They remain unchanged by time and still have their decorative house signs. Rudolf II's choleric astronomer Tycho Brahe (see p43) lived at No. 1 and apparently found the noise of nearby church bells insufferable.

A Bronzino painting, Sternberg Palace

STAG MOAT

When the Stag Moat was not fulfilling its defensive duties, Prague's rulers used it as a hunting park. Rudolf II is said to have been particularly fond of chasing deer around the narrow, wooded gorge with his pet lions. The Powder Bridge's earthworks were excavated to permit pedestrians access to both halves of the moat.

7 Sternberg Palace

This fine Baroque building, dating from 1698, houses the National Gallery's collection of European art from the classical to the Baroque. Spread over three floors, it is without doubt the country's best collection from the period. Its highlights include works by Rubens, Rembrandt and El Greco (see p46).

8 Old Castle Steps
MAP D2

The comparatively gentle slope of the Staré zámecké schody – the castle's "back door" entrance – leads from the Malostranská metro to the citadel's eastern gate. Local artists and artisans line the steps, selling everything from watercolour prints to polished stones.

Charming houses lining tranquil Nový Svět

Archbishop's Palace

9 Hradčanské náměstí
MAP B2

Many visitors enter this square backwards, trying to fit St Vitus's spires into their photographs. Tear your eyes away from the castle's western face and you'll see, among other Renaissance buildings, the colourful Archbishop's Palace and the Schwarzenberg Palace opposite, housing the Bohemian Baroque art of the National Gallery *(see p46)*. In the green centre is a plague column from 1726; opposite the castle is the Toskánský Palace, now part of the Ministry of Foreign Affairs.

10 Radnické schody
MAP B2

The Courthouse Steps lead from Hradčany's former mayoral residence, now the hotel Zlatá Hvězda, to the old courthouse at Loretánská 1. At the bottom are two statues – on the left is St John of Nepomuk and on the right St Joseph with the infant Jesus in Renaissance garb. There are more steps than is immediately apparent, making the pub halfway up a convenient stopping-off point.

Radnické Steps

A DAY IN HRADČANY

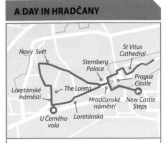

▶ MORNING

Start your day with a brisk climb up the **New Castle Steps**, and time your ascent to hear the 10am Castle Guard brass quartet. After a leisurely stroll through the scenic grounds, leave the castle behind and walk west through **Hradčanské náměstí**. Head to the imposing Schwarzenberg Palace, set amid the Renaissance structures that surround the square, and take time to admire some Baroque Czech art. Alternatively, treat yourself to the Old Masters collection at **Sternberg Palace**.

Now walk up **Loretánská** to **Loretánské náměstí**, where you'll find the vast Černín Palace staring down at The Loreto *(see p101)*. Explore the pilgrimage site and its odd gallery of saints before having lunch at the simple Kavárna Nový Svět *(see p105)*.

AFTERNOON

Exit Loretánské náměstí past the Capuchin monastery and follow Černínská downhill, pausing on **Nový Svět** lane. Coo over the street's charming piebald houses and follow Kanovnická street back to Hradčanské náměstí.

The rest of the afternoon will be taken up with a tour of the unmissable **Prague Castle** *(see p101)*, **St Vitus Cathedral** *(see p101)* and the myriad of other attractions in the castle complex.

To end your sightseeing day in Hradčany, find your way back to the famed pub **U Černého vola** *(see p104)* at Loretánské náměstí 1 for a pickled sausage and a generous mug of beer.

See map on pp100–101 ←

Cafés and Pubs

Exterior of the U Černého vola pub

1 U Černého vola
MAP A2 ■ Loretánské nám. 1

Part of the proceeds from the pub "At the Black Ox" go to the nearby school for the blind. Watching the regulars knock back litres of beer, you can guess why it's so popular.

2 The Strahov Monastic Brewery
MAP A3 ■ Strahovské nádvoří 301

Located in the Strahov Monastery founded by Vladislav II in 1142, this restored brewery has a capacity for 350 guests, split between the courtyard, restaurant and brewery.

3 Na Baště
MAP B2 ■ Zahrada na Baště, Prague Castle

An out-of-the-way, peaceful café in the Gardens on the Bastion, which were designed by Slovenian architect Jože Plečnik, where you can rest over tea or coffee and light snacks.

4 Starbucks Pražský hrad
MAP B2 ■ Ke Hradu

Sip an espresso on the rooftop while peering at Prague through one of the telescopes. The quiet patio has large tables where you can lunch and plan your visit to the castle next door.

5 U Labutí
MAP B2 ■ Hradčanské nám. 11

The pub "At the Swans" serves up Pilsner Urquell and some substantial dishes, such as *schnitzel* and goulash, on its garden terrace overlooking the upper Stag Moat.

6 Romantik Hotel U Raka
MAP A2 ■ Černínská 10

The Hotel U Raka at the far western end of Nový Svět is a striking half-timbered building, an unusual sight in the urban Czech Republic. Enjoy a coffee in cosy surroundings – there is an open fire in winter.

7 Café Galerie
MAP B2 ■ Hradčanské nám. 15

Situated in the Sternberg Palace, this is a good spot to enjoy a cup of coffee and a baguette or a light meal after visiting the castle and before heading off to visit the other palaces nearby.

8 Lobkowicz Palace Café
MAP C2 ■ Jiřská 3

This pleasant and smart restaurant offers light lunches and suppers with a view of the city. The café in the courtyard is the place to end your tour of the castle.

Lobkowicz Palace Café balcony

9 Café Gallery
MAP C2 ■ Zlatá ulička u Daliborky 42

Situated in the narrow alleys leading into Golden Lane, this café offers coffees, wine, spirits and sandwiches. Outdoor seating is available in good weather.

10 Café Melvin
MAP A3 ■ Pohořelec 8

Set in a 15th-century house at the beginning of the Royal Route, this café serves a range of beverages, home-made desserts and sandwiches.

Restaurants

PRICE CATEGORIES

For a three-course meal for one with half a bottle of wine (or equivalent meal), taxes and extra charges.

Ⓚ under Kč500 ⒦⒦ Kč500–Kč1,000
⒦⒦⒦ over Kč1,000

1 Hradčany Restaurant
MAP A2 ■ Hotel Savoy, Keplerova 6 ■ 224 302430 ■ ⒦⒦⒦

This fine dining restaurant is one of the best in the country.

2 Peklo
MAP A3 ■ Strahovské nadvoří 1 ■ 220 516652 ■ ⒦⒦

Continental dining in a grotto under the Strahov Monastery. The house speciality, the "stuffed devil's hoof", is worth ordering.

3 U Císařů
MAP B2 ■ Loretánská 5 ■ 220 518484 ■ ⒦⒦⒦

The restaurant "At the Emperors" serves traditional specialities and international favourites. The decor includes fine pewter tableware collections, hunting weapons and blacksmith bellows.

4 U ševce Matouše
MAP A2 ■ Loretánské náměstí 4 ■ 220 514536 ■ ⒦

"At the Cobbler Matouš", in a cosy, low, vaulted room, has made an art of melting cheese on beefsteaks.

5 Malý Buddha
MAP A3 ■ Úvoz 46 ■ 220 513894 ■ No credit cards ■ ⒦

The "Little Buddha" serves a wide range of potent teas and Vietnamese food.

The sign at the Malý Buddha

The entrance to Lví dvůr

6 Lví dvůr
MAP B1 ■ U Prašného mostu 6 ■ 224 372361 ■ ⒦⒦⒦

The rooftop dining room affords incomparable views of St Vitus Cathedral; the beer hall serves a sublime suckling pig.

7 U Zlaté hrušky
MAP B2 ■ Nový Svět 3 ■ 723 764940 ■ ⒦⒦⒦

"At the Golden Pear" serves delicious Continental and Czech game dishes in picturesque Nový Svět.

8 Kavárna Nový Svět
MAP A2 ■ Nový Svět 2 ■ 242 430700 ■ Closed Wed ■ ⒦

Small family café hidden in a picturesque street. Try soup or salad for lunch, or just sit with a good cup of coffee and enjoy the atmosphere.

9 Host Restaurant
MAP B2 ■ Loretánská 15 ■ 728 695793 ■ ⒦⒦⒦

Excellent, stylish dining alongside sweeping views of Petřín Hill and Malá Strana. Accessed by a particularly steep and narrow staircase.

10 Villa Richter
MAP D1 ■ Staré zámecké schody 6 ■ 702 205108 ■ ⒦⒦⒦

With panoramic views of the city and a choice of two restaurants, Villa Richter has it all. While Terra offers well-priced Czech cuisine, the elegant Piano Nobile serves Central European fare.

See map on pp100–101

TOP 10 Josefov

It is impossible to date precisely the arrival of the Jews in Prague, but historical sources make mention of the destruction of a Jewish settlement on the Vltava's left bank in the 13th century. For the next 500 years, Prague's Jews were obliged to live in a walled community where the Josefov quarter is today, working, studying and worshipping in the confines of the ghetto. So restricted was their allotted space that they were obliged to bury their dead layer upon layer in the Old Jewish Cemetery. When Emperor Josef II removed these strictures, many Jews left the ghetto, which became a slum occupied by the city's poorest residents. The quarter was razed in the late 19th century, making way for avenues such as Pařížská with its fine Art Nouveau houses. During World War II, the synagogues stored valuables looted from Jewish communities across the Reich. Nearly 80,000 Czech and Moravian Jews perished in the Holocaust (see p31).

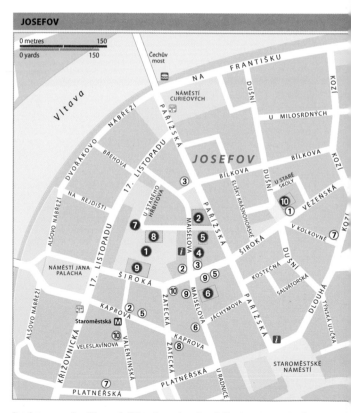

JOSEFOV

Previous pages Small houses built into the castle walls at Golden Lane, Prague Castle

Headstones, Old Jewish Cemetery

1 Old Jewish Cemetery

The sight of hundreds of graves, their leaning headstones crumbling on top of each other, is a moving and unforgettable experience, a testament to the treatment of the Jews in Prague, confined to their own ghetto even in death. Although there is no definite record of the number of burial sites here, to appreciate the depth of the graveyard, compare the gravestones' height with that of the street level on U Starého hřbitova (see pp28–9).

2 Old-New Synagogue

Across the street from the cemetery, Europe's oldest surviving synagogue has witnessed a turbulent history, including pogroms and fire, and has often been a place of refuge for the city's beleaguered Jewish community. Its name (see p48) may come from the fact that another synagogue was built after this one, taking the title "new", but which was later destroyed. It is still the religious centre for Prague's small, present-day Jewish community (see pp30–31).

3 Convent of St Agnes

This lovely 13th-century Gothic convent, now part of the National Gallery, is full of spectacular wall panels and altarpieces, as well as original 13th-century cloisters and chapels. The artworks, part of the gallery's collection, comprise some of the best Czech medieval and early Renaissance art (see pp34–5).

> 1 **Top 10 Sights**
> see pp109–111
>
> 1 **Cafés and Restaurants**
> see p113
>
> 1 **Shops**
> see p112

Vyšší Brod altarpiece at St Agnes

4 Jewish Town Hall
MAP L3 ■ Maiselova 18
■ **Closed to the public**

The hands of the Rococo clock on the town hall, or *Židovská radnice*, turn counterclockwise as Hebrew is read from right to left. The building was one of Mordechai Maisel's gifts to his community in the late 16th century (see p43), but it was renovated in Baroque style in 1763.

Jewish Town Hall

5 High Synagogue
MAP L2 ■ Červená 4 ■ **Closed to the public**

Constructed along with the town hall with funds from Mordechai Maisel, the High Synagogue was built in elegant Renaissance fashion. Subsequent reconstructions updated the exterior, but the interior retains its original stucco vaults. Inside there are also impressive Torah scrolls and mantles.

6 Maisel Synagogue
MAP L3 ■ Maiselova 10 ■ **Open Apr–Oct: 9am–6pm Sun–Fri; Nov–Mar: 9am–4:30pm** ■ **Adm**

Rudolf II gave Mordechai Maisel permission to build his private synagogue here in the late 16th century, in gratitude for the Jewish mayor's financial help in Bohemia's war against the Turks. At the time of its construction it was the largest synagogue in Prague, until fire destroyed it and much of the ghetto in 1689. It was later rebuilt in Neo-Gothic style. Inside is a wonderful collection (see p47) of Jewish silverwork and other items such as candlesticks and ceramics, much of it looted by the Nazis from other synagogues across Bohemia. Ironically, the Third Reich planned to build a museum in Prague, dedicated to the Jews as an "extinct race".

7 Ceremonial Hall
MAP K2 ■ U Starého hřbitova 3a ■ **Open Apr–Oct: 9am–6pm Sun–Fri; Nov–Mar: 9am–4:30pm** ■ **Adm**

Constructed in the early 1900s in striking mock Romanesque fashion, the Ceremonial Hall was home to the Jewish community's Burial Society. The fascinating exhibits housed inside detail the complex Jewish rituals for preparing the dead for the grave.

Early 20th-century Ceremonial Hall

8 Klausen Synagogue
MAP K2 ■ U Starého hřbitova 1
■ **Open Apr–Oct: 9am–6pm Sun–Fri; Nov–Mar: 9am–4:30pm** ■ **Adm**

Abutting the Old Jewish Cemetery, this Baroque single-nave building was constructed in 1694 on the site of a school and prayer hall (klausen) where Rabbi Loew taught the *cabala*. Like most synagogues in the area, it now houses Jewish exhibits (see p47), including prints, pointers and manuscripts.

Torah pointer

RABBI JUDAH LOEW BEN BEZALEL

One of Prague's most famed residents, Rabbi Loew ben Bezalel (c. 1520–1609) is associated with numerous local legends but he was also a pioneering pedagogue and a leading Hebrew scholar of the times. Foremost among the myths surrounding Loew is that of the Golem, a clay automaton the rabbi supposedly created to defend the ghetto (see p60).

Vaulted ceilings, Pinkas Synagogue

⑨ Pinkas Synagogue

MAP K3 ■ Široká 3 ■ Open Apr–Oct: 9am–6pm Sun–Fri; Nov–Mar: 9am–4:30pm ■ Adm

After World War II, this 15th-century Gothic building with some early Renaissance features became a monument to the estimated 80,000 Czech and Moravian victims of the Holocaust – the names and dates of all those known to have died either in the Terezín camp or in others across Eastern Europe are written on the wall in a moving memorial. Equally moving is the exhibition (see p47) of writings and paintings made by the children (of whom there were more than 10,000 under the age of 15) confined in Terezín (see p31).

⑩ Spanish Synagogue

MAP M2 ■ Vézeňská 1 ■ Open Apr–Oct: 9am–6pm Sun–Fri; Nov–Mar: 9am–4:30pm ■ Adm

The Moorish interior with its swirling arabesques and stucco decoration gives this synagogue its name. It stands on the site of the Old School, Prague's first Jewish house of worship. František Škroup, composer of the Czech national anthem, was the organist in the mid-19th century. It hosts exhibitions of Jewish history and synagogue silver (see p47).

The Moorish Spanish Synagogue

See map on pp108–9 ←

A DAY IN THE JEWISH QUARTER

▶ **MORNING**

A sobering place to start the day, the Pinkas Synagogue lists Holocaust victims by their home village and name, and helps visitors to appreciate how large the Czech Jewish community once was. Afterwards take a stroll through the adjoining Old Jewish Cemetery (see p109), where a guide will help you find significant gravesites. Also worth visiting in this area is the Baroque Klausen Synagogue, with its exhibits on Jewish festivals and family life.

A short walk away, at the end of U Starého hřbitova, is the Old-New Synagogue (see p109), where you'll find treasures like Rabbi Loew's seat. Exiting, note the Jewish Town Hall next door with its Hebrew clock. Just round the corner is Kafka Snob Food (see p113), a delightful place to stop for lunch.

AFTERNOON

After lunch, meander among the antiques shops en route to the Maisel Synagogue, where you'll find the first part of an exhibit on Jewish settlement in Bohemia and Moravia – it continues at the Spanish Synagogue a five-minute walk to the east down Široká.

Refresh yourself at Bakeshop Praha (see p112) around the corner before walking a few minutes northeast to the Convent of St Agnes (see p109) with its exhibits of Czech medieval art.

A truly Josefov-style evening involves a kosher dinner at King Solomon (see p113) near the cemetery and a concert of sacred music at the Spanish Synagogue.

Shops

1 **Spanish Synagogue Gift Shop**

MAP M2 ▪ Vězeňská 1

Exquisite torah pointers, *yarmulkas* (skull caps) and unique gifts, such as a watch in the style of the clock on the Jewish Town Hall *(see p110)*.

2 **Judaica**

MAP L2 ▪ Široká 7

This small shop near the Pinkasova Synagogue is Prague's only Jewish bookshop, and sells books and prints, both secondhand and new, to tourists and locals alike.

3 **Hodinářství (Old Clocks)**

MAP L3 ▪ Maiselova 16

If you have trouble finding this small shop selling old clocks, simply stand at the corner of Maiselova and Široká streets and you'll hear the old cuckoo clock sing.

4 **Granát Turnov**

MAP N2 ▪ Dlouhá 28

Specializing in Bohemian garnet, Granát Turnov is part of Prague's biggest jewellery chain. Jewellery lovers can find a large variety of brooches and necklaces here.

5 **Franz Kafka Society Bookshop**

MAP L3 ▪ Široká 12

Works by Franz Kafka in German and in translation, as well as other specialized literature and books on Prague and related subjects can be found here. Guidebooks, souvenirs and gifts can also be purchased.

6 **Studio Šperk**

MAP M2 ▪ Dlouhá 19

Aficionados come to this tiny goldsmith's workshop for eye-catching gold and silver jewellery, much of which is embellished with the celebrated red Bohemian garnet.

The Bakeshop Praha bakery and café

7 **Bakeshop Praha**

MAP M2 ▪ Kozí 1

Grab a bag of brownies, *rugelach* or butterhorns (small crescent-shaped biscuits) and other mouthwatering treats, or lunch on an egg salad sandwich and coffee. There are also salads and quiches to take away.

8 **Antique Kaprova**

MAP L3 ▪ Kaprova 12

This serious collector's shop specializes in prints and small decorative items such as clocks and lamps. If you don't find what you're looking for, just ask and they'll point you in the right direction.

9 **Antique Cinolter**

MAP L3 ▪ Maiselova 9

Art lovers should peruse this small gallery's sale exhibition of local art. The original oils and sketches capture Josefov's bittersweet warmth and humanity.

10 **Alma (Mahlerová) Antique**

MAP K3 ▪ Valentinská 7

What don't they sell? Alma Antique is a bazaar stocked with Persian rugs, jewellery, Meissen porcelain, crystal and ornate nesting dolls. This is one of the largest antique dealers in Prague.

Bohemian garnet ring, Studio Šperk

Cafés and Restaurants

Food for sale at Naše Maso

1 Naše maso
MAP N2 ▪ Dlouhá 39 ▪ 222 312533 ▪ ⓀⓀ

The casual setting in a butcher shop makes this better suited to a quick bite. The meat is quality local beef and pork. Tell them at the counter how you'd like your meat to be done.

2 Paneria
MAP K3 ▪ Kaprova 3 ▪ Ⓚ

Pick up ready-made sandwiches for a picnic on the steps of the nearby Rudolfinum (see p46). Paneria has branches throughout the city.

3 Les Moules
MAP L2 ▪ Pařížská 19 ▪ 222 315022 ▪ ⓀⓀⓀ

This Belgian beer café offers typical brasserie fare along with a variety of seafood dishes. There is also a good selection of French cheeses.

4 Ambroisie Caffè
MAP N3 ▪ Rybná 14 ▪ 221 842121 ▪ Open Mon–Fri ▪ ⓀⓀ

Located in the Burzovní Palace, Ambroisie combines modern design with a lush garden in the atrium. Soups and salads, as well as meat, fish and pasta dishes all feature on the menu.

5 La Bodeguita del Medio
MAP K3 ▪ Kaprova 5 ▪ 224 813922 ▪ ⓀⓀ

This Cuban-Creole restaurant offers grilled fish and meats made using authentic ingredients. Popular with the business crowd, it boasts a great atmosphere and welcoming staff.

6 Pivnice u Pivrnce
MAP L3 ▪ Maiselova 3 ▪ 222 329404 ▪ Ⓚ

A pub with wall decorations by Czech caricaturist Peter Urban. Choose from Czech specialities or enjoy a beer.

7 La Finestra in Cucina
MAP K4 ▪ Platnéřská 90/13 ▪ 222 325325 ▪ ⓀⓀⓀ

Italian favourites cooked to perfection and great wine are complemented by the beautiful setting and good service.

8 Apetit
MAP N2 ▪ Dlouhá 736/23 ▪ 222 329853 ▪ Ⓚ

Try a range of freshwater and marine fish and seafood, plus grilled steaks.

9 Kafka Snob Food
MAP L3 ▪ Široká 12 ▪ 725 915505 ▪ ⓀⓀ

The words "Kafka" and "snob" don't usually go together, but this informal Italian place seems to work well. Perfect for taking a break from sightseeing in the former Jewish quarter.

10 King Solomon
MAP L3 ▪ Široká 8 ▪ 224 818752 ▪ Closed Fri ▪ ⓀⓀⓀ

Prague's foremost kosher restaurant has separate facilities for meat and dairy dishes. Closes for the sabbath.

Conservatory at King Solomon

See map on pp108–9 ←

⁝⁝10 New Town

Founded in 1348, New Town *(Nové Město)* is hardly new. Charles IV's urban development scheme imposed straight avenues on the settlements springing up outside the old city walls and added a fourth town to the constellation of Old Town, Malá Strana and Hradčany. Unlike the Old Town, New Town was a planned grid of streets and markets. The horse market became Wenceslas Square in the 19th century; the 14th-century cattle market, and Europe's largest square, took on Charles's name, becoming Karlovo náměstí. The hay market, Senovážné náměstí, kept its title until the Communists changed it for a time to honour the Russian novelist Maxim Gorky. Since the Velvet Revolution was played out on Národní and Wenceslas Square, these and the surrounding streets have been filled with exciting enterprises.

Lively Wenceslas Square

① Wenceslas Square

This former horse market, in contrast to its medieval counterpart in the Old Town *(see pp18–21)*, expresses the history of 20th-century Prague, from its many beautiful Art Nouveau façades to the memories of the numerous marches, political protests and celebrations that have shaped the city over the past 100 years *(see pp36–7)*.

② Na Příkopě

MAP N5

Formerly a moat protecting the city's eastern flank, Na Příkopě is Prague's fashion boulevard, counting Gant, Benetton, Korres (the only branch in the Czech Republic) and Guess among its range of big-name stores. Shoppers jam the pedestrian zone and pavement cafés, streaming between the gleaming Myslbek

shopping centre and Slovanský dům, with its 10-screen multiplex cinema. The Hussite firebrand Jan Želivský preached on the site now occupied by another shopping mall, the Černá Růže Palace.

③ Náměstí Republiky
MAP P3

The odd couple of the Art Nouveau Municipal House and the Neo-Gothic Powder Tower are the centrepiece of Náměstí Republiky (Republic Square), facing the Czech National Bank's stern façade and the renovated Hybernia Theatre. Behind the theatre is the former home of the Lenin Museum, which was closed in 1991 after the Communists had lost power. In the northeast corner of the square stands Palladium, a unique shopping mall with the exterior of the former Franciscan Monastery and newly built interior. On the opposite side stands Kotva, a former socialist department store.

Trams at Náměstí Republiky

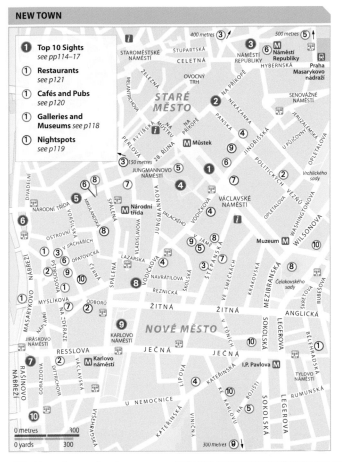

NEW TOWN

1 **Top 10 Sights**
see pp114–17

1 **Restaurants**
see p121

1 **Cafés and Pubs**
see p120

1 **Galleries and
Museums** see p118

1 **Nightspots**
see p119

4 **Franciscan Garden**
MAP N6

The Franciscans moved here in 1604, claiming a former Carmelite monastery. The grounds and nearby Church of Our Lady of the Snow had fallen into decay after the Hussite civil war, but the monks beautifully restored them. The gardens were closed to the public until 1950, when the Communists thought they were worth sharing. Although there's little love lost for the dictatorship of the proletariat, the gardens remain popular with young couples and pigeon-feeding pensioners *(see p53)*.

The tranquil Franciscan Garden

5 Národní třída
MAP L6

The end of Communism in Czechoslovakia began midway between the National Theatre and what is now the Tesco supermarket. On 17 November 1989, police put a brutal end to a pro-democracy march as it made its way down to Wenceslas Square. A plaque at Národní třída 20 marks the spot where the marchers and the truncheons met.

6 National Theatre
MAP E4 ▪ Národní třída 2
▪ www.narodni-divadlo.cz

Patriotic Czechs funded the theatre's construction twice: once in 1868 and again after fire destroyed the building in 1883. To see the stunning allegorical ceiling frescoes and Vojtěch Hynais's celebrated stage curtain, take in one of the operas staged here; good picks are Smetana's *Libuše*, which debuted here, or Dvořák's *The Devil and Kate*. You can see black-light productions at the Laterna Magika next door *(see p66)*.

The grand National Theatre

Gehry and Milunic's Dancing House

7 Dancing House
MAP E6 ▪ Rašínovo nábřeží 80
▪ www.tancici-dum.cz

Built in 1992–6, this edifice by Vlado Milunic and Frank Gehry is known as the Dancing House, or "Ginger and Fred", due to its iconic towers, which resemble two dancers. Most of the building is now a hotel owned by former Czech international football player, Vladimír Šmicer. The two tower rooms, with their castle and Vltava views, are among the best in the capital.

8 New Town Hall
MAP F5 ▪ Karlovo náměstí 23
▪ Tower open Apr–Nov 10am–6pm
Tue–Sun ▪ Adm ▪ www.nrpraha.cz

In 1419, an anti-clerical mob led by Jan Želivský hurled the Catholic mayor and his councillors from a New Town Hall window in the first of Prague's defenestrations *(see p15)*. The Gothic tower was added a few years later; its viewing platform is open to the public. Crowds gather at the tower's base most Saturdays to congratulate newlyweds married in the building's Gothic hall.

New Town Hall

MŮSTEK

The area at the bottom of Wenceslas Square takes its name from the "Little Bridge" that spanned the moat here in medieval times. Below the surface, at the top of the escalators descending to the train platform, you'll find the remains of that bridge, uncovered by workers building the metro.

⑨ Karlovo náměstí
MAP F5

Charles IV had his city planners build New Town's central square to the same dimensions as Jerusalem's. Originally a cattle market, it is now a park popular with dog-walkers. Among the trees are monuments to such luminaries as Eliška Krásnohorská, who wrote libretti for Smetana's operas. To the west, on Resslova, is the 18th-century Cathedral of Sts Cyril and Methodius. The Czech resistance fighters who assassinated Nazi leader Reinhard Heydrich (1904–42) took refuge here before their deaths (see p49).

Monument at Palackého náměstí

⑩ Palackého náměstí
MAP E6

The riverside square is named for the 19th-century historian František Palacký, whose work was integral to the National Revival. Stanislav Sucharda's sweeping monument to him stands at the plaza's northern end, while the modern steeples of the Emaus Monastery rise from the eastern edge (see p61). The church grounds are also known as the Slavonic Monastery, named after the liturgy the resident Balkan Benedictines used. Sadly, American bombs demolished the monastery's original Baroque steeples in 1945 on St Valentine's Day, as part of the Allies' World War II campaign.

A DAY IN NEW TOWN

(map showing: Museum of Communism, Národní třída, Wenceslas Square, National Theatre, St Wenceslas Statue, Universal, U Matěje Kotrby, National Museum, Galerie Mánes, Sts Cyril and Methodius, U Havrana, Dancing House, Radost FX)

▶ **MORNING**

Head to **Wenceslas Square** (see p114) to begin the day's sightseeing. Start with a quick look at the **National Museum** (see p118) at the top of the square. The nation's leading natural history museum is closed until 2018 but its grand façade still dominates the square. Walk to **St Wenceslas's statue** and the monument to Communism's victims. Get in a bit of retail therapy as you stroll north to Můstek, then visit the **Museum of Communism** (see p118), located, ironically, above McDonald's and a casino. Then walk 10 minutes west down stately **Národní třída** towards the river for lunch at **Universal** (see p121).

AFTERNOON

A short walk to the river and north along its banks leads you to the **National Theatre** for a glimpse at its magnificent façade. Then follow the Vltava south. Modern-art buffs should stop at **Galerie Mánes** (see p118) on the way. Further south, pause at Jiráskovo náměstí to admire the iconic Post-Modern **Dancing House**. Then turn left and follow Resslova uphill to the **Cathedral of Sts Cyril and Methodius** and leafy Karlovo náměstí.

Take in a performance at the National Theatre in the evening; **U Matěje Kotrby** (see p120) is the obvious choice for dinner, before or after. If you still have the energy, head to **Radost FX** (see p119) to dance the night away or to **U Havrana** (see p120) with its local, smoky atmosphere.

See map on p115 ←

Galleries and Museums

Galerie Mánes on the Vltava

1 Galerie Mánes
MAP E5 ■ Masarykovo nábřeží 250 ■ Open 10am–6pm Tue–Sun ■ Adm

Occupying the southern tip of Žofín Island, this contemporary art gallery hosts both Czech and foreign artists.

2 Galerie Via Art
MAP E6 ■ Resslova 6 ■ Open 1–6pm Mon–Thu, 1–5pm Fri ■ www.galerieviaart.com

Founded in 1991 as one of Prague's first private galleries, Galerie Via Art exhibits contemporary painting, sculpture and mixed-media art and arranges artist exchanges.

3 Postal Museum
MAP G1 ■ Nové mlýny 2 ■ Open 9am–noon, 1–5pm Tue–Sun ■ Adm ■ www.postovni muzeum.cz

Philatelists' mouths water over this one. Its exhibitions illustrate the colourful history of postage stamps in the Czech Republic and Europe. Sells commemorative sheets and graphic works too.

4 Mucha Museum
MAP P5 ■ Panská 7 ■ Open 10am–6pm daily ■ Adm ■ www.mucha.cz

Art Nouveau artist Alfons Mucha is a national hero. Here you'll find his journals, sketchbooks and paintings, both private and commercial.

5 Prague City Museum
MAP H2 ■ Na Poříčí 52 ■ Open 9am–6pm Tue–Sun ■ Adm ■ en.muzeumprahy.cz

Visitors can explore 19th-century Prague with Antonín Langweil's scaled replica of the city.

6 Museum of Communism
MAP N5 ■ V Celnici 4 ■ Open 9am–8pm daily ■ Adm ■ muzeumofcommunism.com

A triptych of the dream, reality and nightmare that was Communist Czechoslovakia. The museum is filled with mementos of the nation's past.

7 Václav Špála Gallery
MAP L6 ■ Národní třída 30 ■ Open 11am–7pm daily ■ www.spalovka.cz

This contemporary gallery exhibits works mainly by local artists and aims to make art more accessible.

8 National Museum
MAP G5 ■ Václavské náměstí 68 ■ Closed for refurbishment until 2018 ■ Adm ■ www.nm.cz

Its collections are scattered across the city and country, but this imposing building is a cultural artifact in its own right (see p46).

Art, Mucha Museum

9 Police Museum
MAP G7 ■ Ke Karlovu 1 ■ Open 10am–5pm Tue–Sun ■ Adm ■ muzeumpolicie.cz

Engaging exhibits, such as an interactive crime scene, document the history of the police.

10 Dvořák Museum
MAP G6 ■ Ke Karlovu 20 ■ Open 10am–5pm Tue–Sun ■ Adm ■ www.nm.cz

This Baroque palace houses the composer's piano and viola, as well as other memorabilia (see p44).

Nightspots

 1 Radost FX
MAP G6 ■ Bělehradská 120

Late at night, club kids take over the disco, lounge and café. By day, a broader demographic comes in for the good vegetarian food. Sunday brunch is especially popular. Open until 4am *(see p68)*.

The bar area at Radost FX

2 La Loca
MAP E5 ■ Odborů 278/4

Enjoy excellent cocktails, varied cuisine and free music entertainment at this trendy international music bar and lounge. Happy hours are between 6pm and 8pm.

3 Jazz Republic
MAP M6 ■ Jilská 1a

One of Prague's top music clubs, Jazz Republic features live jazz, funk, blues, dance, Latin, fusion or world music seven nights a week. The programme varies every month.

 4 Lucerna Music Bar
The granddaddy of Prague's clubs, the cavernous Lucerna hosts live jazz as well as rock and dance parties, including the ever popular 1980s and 1990s nights *(see p69)*.

5 Escape Club
MAP F4 ■ V Jámě 8

If you want to step out for drinks and meet interesting people, then this gay club is the perfect place. Expect oil shows, striptease performances, dance shows, drinking games and much more.

6 Reduta Jazz Club
MAP L6 ■ Národní třída 20

Many celebrated musicians have played here, as has former US President Bill Clinton. Visit to hear all types of jazz from swing bands to modern styles.

7 Duplex Dine & Dance
MAP N6 ■ Václavské nám. 21

During the day, Duplex is an ideal location for lunch or dinner with good views of the city. At night it turns into one of Prague's most exclusive clubs.

8 Ultramarin
MAP E4 ■ Ostrovní 32

The ground floor is a simple, convivial bar and restaurant. After you've had your fill, you'll find a music club downstairs where you can dance. Open until 4am.

9 Billiard centrum v Cípu
MAP N5 ■ V Cípu 1

Close to 100 billiard, pool and snooker tables, plus four lanes of bowling and two table-tennis sets. If you're planning on going on Friday or Saturday, it is best to make a reservation – this place can get crowded. The bar serves drinks only.

10 Nebe (Heaven)
MAP E5 ■ Křemencova 10

This atmospheric club in an original stone cellar features stylish lighting and a gracefully curvaceous long bar. A separate lounge is a popular place for various private events.

Partygoers at Nebe

See map on p115

Cafés and Pubs

Globe Bookstore and Café

1 Globe Bookstore and Café
MAP E5 ▪ Pštrossova 6 ▪ 224 934203

The quality of the food varies with the Globe's mercurial staff. The best time to visit is weekend brunch.

2 Solidní Jistota
MAP E5 ▪ Pštrossova 21

This place serves excellent Moravian wines, plus a wide array of spirits and cocktails. At night the bar transforms into a nightclub.

3 Café 35
MAP F5 ▪ Štěpánská 35

Students at the Institut Français and other Francophones gather here for coffee, quiche and a quiet read of the French newspapers. The garden is a peaceful spot on sunny days.

4 Novoměstský Pivovar
MAP F5 ▪ Vodičkova 20 ▪ 222 232448

Enter this great place to expand your knowledge of beer and try classic Czech dishes in a working brewery.

5 Hostinec U Kalicha
MAP G6 ▪ Na bojišti 12–14

This pub's decor and cartooned walls are based on the Czech novel *The Good Soldier Švejk*. Author Jaroslav Hašek (*see p44*) set some of the pivotal scenes here.

6 U Matěje Kotrby
MAP E5 ▪ Křemencova 1738/17 ▪ 224 930768

This lovely bar and restaurant with an old-world feel serves Czech-style meals, cold Pilsner and local wines.

7 Rocky O'Reilly's
MAP F5 ▪ Štěpánská 32

Offering all a Celtophile could ask for, this pub has live music in the evenings, football on the TV, a roaring fire and plenty of stout. The food's decent as well.

8 Café Louvre
MAP L6 ▪ Národní třída 20

Franz Kafka, Max Brod and their writer friends used to hold court here. It's a bright, cheerful place, good for conversation and grabbing a bite to eat. At the back is Prague's classiest pool hall.

The exterior of U Fleků

9 U Fleků
MAP E5 ▪ Křemencova 11

Exactly what you might expect from the city that created the "Beer-Barrel Polka". U Fleků is the city's oldest brewing pub, dating to 1499, and probably the most popular, and the prices reflect it. It is known for its dark lager (*see p74*).

10 U Havrana
MAP G5 ▪ Hálkova 6

One of a dying breed, the Raven serves premium Kozel beer and some of the best greasy food in town. It is open until 5am.

Restaurants

1 Dynamo
MAP E5 ■ Pštrossova 29 ■ 224 932020 ■ ⓚ

This Post-Modern diner serves dishes such as rump steak in marinade with thyme and oregano. A wide selection of vegetarian options is on offer.

2 Restaurace Bredovský dvůr
MAP P6 ■ Politických vězňů 13 ■ ⓚⓚ

Enjoy traditional Czech dishes such as game goulash with Carlsbad dumplings. In the summer, you can eat alfresco.

3 Universal
MAP E5 ■ V Jirchářích 6 ■ 224 934416 ■ ⓚⓚ

A popular eatery, serving substantial meals at moderate prices. The café is especially recommended for its vegetarian dishes.

4 U Emy Destinnové
MAP F6 ■ Kateřinská 7 ■ Closed Sun ■ 224 918425 ■ ⓚⓚⓚ

Named for a famous Czech opera diva, the restaurant is a labour of love for the American owner and chef Steven Trumpfheller. The eatery's seasonal menu focuses on high-quality seafood, Black Angus steaks and unusual game dishes. The elegant setting suits a special night out.

5 U Pinkasů
MAP M6 ■ Jungmannovo náměstí 16 ■ 221 111152 ■ ⓚⓚ

A great-value Czech beer hall since 1843, this is a very popular lunchtime destination. Food is simple but hearty, and the atmosphere lively.

6 Modrý Zub
MAP N6 ■ Jindřišská 5 ■ 222 212622 ■ ⓚⓚ

This is fast Thai food at its best, great for a quick snack or light meal. Huge windows create a great opportunity for people watching.

PRICE CATEGORIES
For a three-course meal for one with half a bottle of wine (or equivalent meal), taxes and extra charges.
....
ⓚ under Kč500 ⓚⓚ Kč500–Kč1,000
ⓚⓚⓚ over Kč1,000

7 Lemon Leaf
MAP E5 ■ Myslíkova 14 ■ 224 919056 ■ ⓚⓚ

Thai and Burmese specials. The ingredients used are fresh, the presentation colourful and service is fast and friendly.

8 Jáma Restaurace
MAP F4 ■ V jámě 7 ■ 222 967081 ■ ⓚⓚ

Delicious Tex-Mex and American specialities and a fun atmosphere. Watch sporting events on plasma screens dotted around the room.

9 Room
MAP F4 ■ V Jámě 6 ■ 221 634103 ■ ⓚⓚ

The house restaurant of the Icon Hotel & Lounge offers inventive, high-quality tapas dishes, along with very good local and foreign wines in an upbeat, contemporary setting.

The sleek decor at Room

10 Čestr
MAP G5 ■ Legerova 75 ■ 222 727851 ■ ⓚⓚⓚ

This is the perfect gourmet dinner choice before or after a night at the State Opera. The traditional beef steaks are delicious.

See map on p115

🔟 Greater Prague

Prague's city centre can keep most visitors occupied for days, but if you're staying outside the city's heart, or if you have the time to explore beyond the capital's walls, the outlying areas offer plenty of surprises. Over the centuries, the various rulers of Prague have used the surrounding countryside as their personal playground, building impressive castles, palaces and parks to which they could escape the often claustrophobic streets and winding alleyways of the city. Even the Communists have left their own kind of functional mark on the area, with useful edifices, towers and exhibition spaces.

From the peaceful parklands of Vyšehrad and the social atmosphere of Letná, to the rowdy nightlife of Žižkov and the intriguing gardens of Holešovice and Troja, Greater Prague has a diversity that will fulfil almost any requirements you might have.

Smetana's grave, Vyšehrad

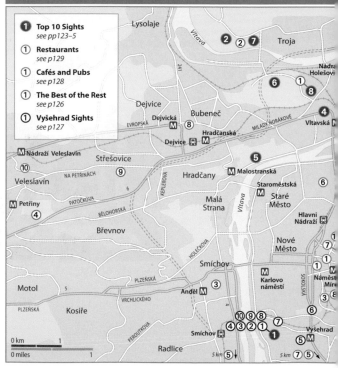

AREA MAP OF GREATER PRAGUE

1 Top 10 Sights
see pp123–5

1 Restaurants
see p129

1 Cafés and Pubs
see p128

1 The Best of the Rest
see p126

1 Vyšehrad Sights
see p127

1 Vyšehrad
MAP B6

The former fortress of Vyšehrad *(see p127)* is steeped in legend. Bedřich Smetana paid tribute to the second seat of the Přemyslid dynasty that resided here in the 10th century in his opera *Libuše* and in his rousing work *Má vlast (see p45)*. He is buried here in the National Cemetery, as are many other Czech luminaries.

2 Prague Zoo
MAP B5 ■ U Trojského zámku 120, Troja ■ Check online for opening times ■ Adm ■ www.zoopraha.cz

Prague's popular zoological gardens date back to 1931. Spread across a vast area, the zoo is home to a number of bird and animal species, including probably the world's largest Giant Salamander.

Church of St Ludmila, Vinohrady

3 Vinohrady
MAP C6

Originally the royal vineyards, Vinohrady today is a gently rolling residential neighbourhood. The central square, Náměstí Míru, features the Neo-Gothic Church of St Ludmila and the Art Nouveau Vinohrady Theatre. For a bit of peace and greenery visit the Havlíčkovy sady.

4 Holešovice
MAP B5

Developers are helping this former warehouse district make a comeback. It is home to the National Gallery's Trade Fair Palace *(see pp32–3)*, which holds the gallery's collection of modern and contemporary art. Motor car enthusiasts will love the National Technical Museum *(see p47)*, with its exhibits of Czech interwar vehicles such as Škodas, as well as other vintage vehicles.

Cars, National Technical Museum

ŽIŽKOV

This working-class neighbourhood came into being when city fathers divided the expanding Královské Vinohrady district. The inhabitants of the area thumbed their noses at Habsburg rule and named their new district after the Hussite warrior. Žižkovites' contrary nature runs deep, even having a separatist movement which promotes an independent Republic of Žižkov. An alternative culture thrives around the Akropolis club and the Divus artists collective, and, increasingly, numerous ethnic restaurants are bringing an international flavour to the area.

Letná Park
MAP E1

A grand staircase leads from the Vltava riverbank opposite the Josefov quarter (see pp108–13) to a giant metronome. The needle marks time where a mammoth statue of Joseph Stalin once stood before it was blown up in 1962 (see p50). The surrounding park echoes with the clatter of skateboards and barking dogs. Travelling circuses sometimes set up in the open fields, but Letná's popular beer garden is probably its biggest draw.

Statue in Letná Park

Stromovka
MAP B5

King Ottokar II established the royal game park here in the 13th century; it's been a public garden since 1804 (*stromovka* means "place of trees"). Stroll, skate or simply enjoy the ancient park by day and visit the planetarium by night. The fish ponds

were a creation of Rudolf II – the emperor drilled a tunnel under Letná in the 16th century to bring in water to supply them (see p52).

The classical façade of Troja Château

Troja
MAP B5

The riverside gardens and château of Troja are an excellent destination for a day trip. Cross the Vltava from Stromovka, take in the château's beautiful garden and art collection (see p126), the Baroque chapel of St Clare and the Prague Zoo. There is a bus from here that will take you to the nearest metro station (Nádraží Holešovice).

Výstaviště
MAP B5

The fairgrounds here were originally built at the end of the 19th century to host trade shows, which are still held at the Industrial Palace and Křižík's Pavilions. There's an amusement park with rides for the kids, an indoor swimming pool, an ice-hockey rink at the Tipsport Arena and the oddly charming musical Křižík Fountain (see p63). If you want to see the original statues that graced Charles Bridge, pay a visit to the Lapidárium, where they are preserved (see p126). A visit to the country's largest aquarium, Mořský Svět, is an excellent option on a rainy day.

National Memorial on the Vítkov Hill

(9) National Memorial on the Vítkov Hill

MAP C6 ■ Žižkov ■ Open 10am–6pm Wed–Sun ■ Adm

The one-eyed Hussite general Jan Žižka defeated invading crusaders in 1420 atop the hill where his giant equestrian statue now stands in front of the Tomb of the Unknown Soldier. Erected in 1929, the monument serves as a memorial to all those who suffered in the Czech struggle for independence. The Communists co-opted the building, and for a time it served as President Klement Gottwald's mausoleum (see p50).

(10) Žižkov TV Tower

MAP C6 ■ Mahlerovy sady ■ Open 8am–midnight ■ Adm

The Communists unashamedly cleared away a Jewish cemetery on the site in the 1970s to make way for this eyesore, reaching 216 m (709 ft) in height. However it didn't begin transmitting until after the Velvet Revolution (see p43). Despite a viewing platform, the tower is actually too tall to see anything clearly, but thrill-seekers may want to try (see p50).

Žižkov TV Tower

THREE AFTERNOON WALKS

AFTERNOON ONE

See **Vyšehrad** (see p123) late in the day, but only if the weather looks promising. Take the metro to the Vyšehrad stop at the **Congress Centre** (see p127), from where you have marvellous views of Prague's spires. Walk west along Na Bučance and enter the fortifications through the **Tábor Gate** (see p127). Once inside the walls, you'll find historic constructions everywhere you turn, such as the lovely Romanesque **Rotunda of St Martin** (see p127). Enjoy the park at your leisure but get to the westernmost edge of the compound atop Vyšehrad's rocky outcrop in time for sunset.

AFTERNOON TWO

Žižkov and **Vinohrady** (see p123) are also best seen in the second half of the day. From Florenc metro, climb to the **National Memorial on the Vítkov Hill** for a wonderful view, then compare it to the one you get from the **Žižkov TV Tower**. Take a stroll as far into Vinohrady as your feet will permit you, but save your strength: you'll need it for a night out pubbing and clubbing.

AFTERNOON THREE

Energetic and keen walkers can manage to see **Stromovka** and **Troja** in half a day. Take the tram to **Výstaviště**, among the trees of the former game park, before crossing the Vltava to the **Troja Château** (see p126). From there, you're within easy walking distance of **Prague Zoo** (see p123). Take bus 112 back to the metro at Nádraží Holešovice.

See map on pp122–3 ←

The Best of the Rest

Late 19th-century Lapidárium

1 Lapidárium
MAP B5 ▪ Výstaviště 422, Holešovice ▪ Check online for opening times ▪ Adm ▪ www.nm.cz

This is where Prague's statues go when they retire. The 700-plus items include the original St Wenceslas.

2 Troja Château
MAP B5 ▪ U Trojského zámku 1, Troja ▪ Check online for opening times ▪ Adm ▪ en.ghmp.cz

Jean-Baptiste Mathey created Count Sternberg's 17th-century palace in Classical Italian style. It has a 19th-century Czech art collection (see p46).

3 Smíchov
MAP B6

This used to be the city's main industrial centre. Anděl metro station still bears traces of its Communist origins (see p51).

4 Břevnov Monastery
MAP A6 ▪ Markétská 28, Břevnov ▪ Check online for tour times ▪ Adm ▪ www.brevnov.cz

St Adalbert founded this Benedictine monastery in 993. You can see the remains of a Romanesque and an 18th-century church.

5 Barrandov Studios
MAP B7 ▪ Kříženeckého náměstí 5, Barrandov ▪ 267 071111 ▪ Open by appt ▪ www.barrandov.cz

Once a Nazi and Communist propaganda mill, today the studios are thriving as western film-makers discover the benefits of filming in Prague.

6 Olšany Cemetery
MAP C6 ▪ Vinohradská 153 ▪ Open Mar, Apr, Oct: 8am–6pm; May–Sep: 8am–7pm; Nov–Feb: 8am–5pm

Plague victims were interred here when the site was still far from the city. Other notable residents include Jan Palach (see p36).

7 Kafka's Grave
MAP C6 ▪ Izraelská 1 ▪ Open Apr–Oct: 9am–5pm Sun–Thu, 9am–2pm Fri; Nov–Mar: 9am–4pm Sun–Thu, 9am–2pm Fri

Kafka's sombre gravemarker lies close to the entrance along Row 21 at the New Jewish Cemetery.

8 Church of the Most Sacred Heart of Our Lord
MAP C6 ▪ Nám. Jiřího z Poděbrad, Vinohrady

Designed by Slovenian architect Josip Plečnik, this modern building was inspired by old Christian architecture.

9 Villa Müller
MAP B6 ▪ Nad Hradním vodojemem 14 ▪ 224 312012 ▪ www.muzeumprahy.cz/mullerova-vila

A masterpiece of avant-garde architecture, this villa by Adolf Loos is a fusion of Functionalism and old English-style design. Reservations needed.

10 DOX Centre for Contemporary Art
MAP C5 ▪ Poupětova 1, Holešovice ▪ Check online for opening times ▪ Adm ▪ www.dox.cz

Housed in a former factory, this multifunctional space presents contemporary international art, architecture and design.

DOX Centre for Contemporary Art

Vyšehrad Sights

 Sts Peter and Paul Cathedral
Štulcova ▪ Metro Vyšehrad ▪ Open Apr–Oct: 10am–6pm; Nov–Mar: 10am–5pm

Although the first church to stand on this site was founded by Vratislav II in the 11th century, the Neo-Gothic structure seen today dates from 1903. The very valuable Gothic altar with a panel depicting *Our Lady of the Rains* is on the right-hand side of the chapel.

 Slavín Monument
K Rotundě ▪ Metro Vyšehrad ▪ Open Jan, Feb, Nov, Dec: 8am–5pm; Mar, Apr, Oct: 8am–6pm; May–Sep: 8am–7pm

This is the burial place of several notable Czech cultural figures. Students laid flowers in remembrance here on 17 November 1989, before marching into town for the Velvet Revolution (see p43).

Slavín Monument

3 **Devil's Pillar**
K Rotundě ▪ Metro Vyšehrad

The story goes that the devil bet a local priest that he could carry this pillar from the Church of St Mary to Rome before the clergyman could finish his sermon. Being a sore loser, Satan threw the column he was carrying to the ground here.

4 **Tábor Gate (Špička)**
V Pevnosti ▪ Metro Vyšehrad

Charles IV restored Vyšehrad's fortifications in the 14th century. Catholic crusaders rode through this gate on their way to crush the Táborites in 1434.

5 **Congress Centre**
Metro Vyšehrad

This ex-Communist palace of culture now hosts international conferences as well as – thanks to its excellent acoustics – pop concerts (see p50).

 Nusle Bridge
Metro Vyšehrad

This simple, utilitarian viaduct spans the Nusle Valley, connecting New Town to the Pankrác banking and commercial district.

7 **Cubist Houses**
Metro Vyšehrad

Czech architect Josef Chochol (1880–1956) built these angular masterpieces in 1913 on Rašínovo nábřeží, Libušina and the corner of Přemyslova and Neklanova streets.

 Smetana's Grave
Metro Vyšehrad

At the start of each year's Prague Spring International Music Festival (see p80), musicians attend a ceremony at composer Bedřich Smetana's grave.

9 **Casemates**
Metro Vyšehrad

In the 18th century, occupying French troops drilled niches in Vyšehrad rock to store ammunition.

10 **Rotunda of St Martin**
K Rotundě ▪ Metro Vyšehrad

This 11th-century chapel is the oldest in Prague and most likely to be the oldest Christian house of worship in the country. It was reconstructed in 1878.

The simple Rotunda of St Martin

See map on pp122–3

Cafés and Pubs

1 Kavárna Pražírna
MAP G6 ■ Lublaňská 676/50, Vinohrady ■ 720 385622
■ www.kavarnaprazirna.cz

Enjoy the flavour and aroma of freshly roasted Arabica coffees at this brick-lined café. Also try the home-made desserts and pickled cheese.

2 U Vystřeleného Oka
MAP C6 ■ U Božích bojovníků 3, Žižkov

The name "At the Shot-Out Eye" is a tribute to the half-blind Hussite general Jan Žižka from whom Žižkov takes its name and whose enormous statue looms overhead (see p125).

U Vystřeleného Oka sign

3 U Holanů
MAP H7 ■ Londýnská 10, Vinohrady

Tuck into a plate of pickled sausages or herring at Vinohrady's favourite no-nonsense pub. Simple but clean, with perfunctory service; they don't make them like this anymore.

4 U Houdků
MAP C6 ■ Bořivojova 110, Žižkov ■ 222 711239 ■ No credit cards

This hidden little gem in Žižkov serves Czech meals that are great value for money. In summer you can sit outside.

5 Hospůdka nad Viktorkou
MAP C6 ■ Bořivojova 79, Žižkov

Bořivojova street boasts more pubs per metre than any other place in the country, and quite possibly the world. There's nothing elegant about Hospůdka nad Viktorkou, but it's the ultimate Prague pub.

6 Café Imperial
MAP G2 ■ Na Poříčí 15, Prague 1

Creative cooking is served at this eatery, which also offers a special Czech menu selection, breakfast and daily lunch specials.

7 Café Faux Pas
MAP H5 ■ Vinohradská 31, Vinohrady ■ www.cafe-fauxpas.cz

Start the day at this café which opens at 8am and serves up a variety of sweet and savoury crêpes and fresh sandwiches.

8 Hlučná samota
MAP H7 ■ Zahřebská 14, Vinohrady

This refined pub takes its name from Bohumil Hrabal's 1976 short novel *Too Loud a Solitude (see p45)*. Neither loud nor solitary, this pub offers its guests excellent food and beer, for which they loyally return every time.

9 Můj šálek kávy
MAP B5 ■ Křižíkova 105, Karlín ■ 725 556944 ■ www.mujsalekkavy.cz

Sip away at speciality coffee and savour home-made cakes and cookies at the flagship café of Czech double-shot coffee roasters. The interesting decor includes bare walls, books and artwork.

10 Pastička
MAP B6 ■ Blanická 25, Vinohrady

The Mousetrap is a perfect blend of old-fashioned beer hall and modish gastropub. Visit it for a choice of light and semi-dark Bernard beer, good, filling food and eclectic Irish decor.

Pastička gastropub

Restaurants

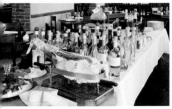

The dining room at Aromi

PRICE CATEGORIES

For a three-course meal for one with half a bottle of wine (or equivalent meal), taxes and extra charges.

Ⓚ under Kč500 ⓀⓀ Kč500–Kč1,000
ⓀⓀⓀ over Kč1,000

1 Aromi

MAP H5 ■ Náměstí Míru 6, Prague 2 ■ 222 713222 ■ ⓀⓀⓀ

This excellent Italian restaurant serves up a fantastic menu of authentic food accompanied by an extensive range of wines from all the world.

2 Olympos

MAP C6 ■ Kubelíkova 9, Žižkov ■ 222 722239 ■ ⓀⓀ

Prague's best Greek food is on offer here. The large garden, complete with table tennis, is ideal for summer dining. The mixed salad platter is the best value around.

3 Mailsi

MAP C6 ■ Lipanská 1, Žižkov ■ 222 717783 ■ No credit cards ■ ⓀⓀ

This little Pakistani eatery offers better value than the Indian restaurants in the centre. Located close to the No. 9 tram stop, it's not as remote as it appears.

4 Rana

MAP C5 ■ Na Dědince 12, Palmovka ■ 721 809084 ■ No credit cards ■ Ⓚ

When Mehfooz Ahmed sold Mailsi to his brother, his fans followed him here, where he serves up the best curries in town. The vindaloo is for true spice devotees.

5 Koliba Praha

MAP C7 ■ Gregorova 8, Horní Roztyly ■ 272 941340 ■ ⓀⓀ

Visitors and locals alike enjoy traditional Czech and Slovak specialities and a good choice of wines. At the weekend, evenings are enlivened by a Romany band.

6 Hotel Diana

Slévačská 496/48, Prague 9 ■ 724 854223 ■ Closed D, Sun ■ ⓀⓀ

It's a trek getting here, but this wins the prize for the best game restaurant. The dill-and-potato *kulajda* soup is a must. Try the boar, too. The dress code is formal.

7 Restaurant Villa Voyta

K Novému dvoru 124/54, Prague 4 ■ 261 711307 ■ ⓀⓀ

Artist Mikoláš Aleš *(see p19)* was an early guest of the original 1912 Daliborka inn. Today's diners are offered traditional European and Czech cuisine indoors or under the ancient chestnut trees in the garden.

8 U Cedru

MAP B5 ■ Národní Obrany 27, Dejvice ■ 233 342974 ■ ⓀⓀ

For an authentic Lebanese dining experience, order pitta with hummus, tabbouleh and other appetizers.

9 Máneska

MAP C6 ■ Mánesova 59, Vinohrady ■ 222 212052 ■ ⓀⓀ

Steaks, salads, ribs and other American dishes keep tables full. The menu changes regularly. Reservations are a must.

10 U Marčanů

MAP A6 ■ Veleslavínská 14, Prague 6 ■ 235 360623 ■ Ⓚ

Folk music and dancing make this a fun lunch spot. Large portions of Czech food are served at communal tables. Book ahead and take a taxi.

See map on pp122–3 ←

Streetsmart

Colourful old buildings in the historic
Prague quarter of Malá Strana

Getting To and Around Prague	**132**
Practical Information	**134**
Places to Stay	**140**
General Index	**148**
Acknowledgments	**156**
Phrase Book	**159**

Getting To and Around Prague

Arriving by Air

Václav Havel Airport Prague (PRG), 16 km (10 miles) northwest of the city centre, is Prague's only international airport. Terminal 2 serves the Schengen zone: mainly Switzerland and Continental EU countries. Terminal 1 serves other destinations, including the UK and Ireland. The airport is well served by international airlines, with direct connections to major European cities, plus many Middle Eastern cities. There are normally no direct flights to North America, although **Czech Airlines** (ČSA) and **Delta** sometimes offer flights to New York (JFK) or Atlanta over Christmas and summer holidays. Travellers from the UK should check **EasyJet**, **Ryanair**, **Smartwings** or **Wizz Air** for inexpensive fares. Direct flights from London take 2 hours, and 9 hours from New York.

Both the terminals are modern, well-maintained structures, with shops, restaurants, ATMs, car rental offices and tourist information booths.

They are both connected by buses, minibuses and taxis to the town centre. Prague Public Transit bus No. 119 runs regularly from 5am to 11pm and departs from just outside the arrivals area of both terminals. Take it to the line's last station, Nádraží Veleslavín, then switch to metro line A into the city centre. Tickets (Kč32, good for both the bus and metro)

can be bought at public transport booths inside the terminals, or from orange ticket vending machines (have local currency handy). Another option is the AE bus to the main railway station (60Kč – tickets from the driver). Taxis line outside the arrivals halls of both terminals and cost about Kč650 to the centre.

Arriving by Rail

Major European rail routes serve Prague, and international trains to the city are comfortable and a good alternative to flying, with couchette sleeping facilities. Most international trains arrive at **Prague Main Railway Station** (Praha hlavní nádraží), which is also on metro line C. It has shops, restaurants, ATMs, left luggage facilities and a taxi stand, and is 10 minutes on foot from Wenceslas Square.

Arriving by Road

Buses are well priced, comfortable and your best option for long trips on a budget. Most major international and domestic bus services, including **Eurolines** and **Flixbus**, operate from Prague's **Florenc Bus Terminal**. This lies at the intersection of metro lines B and C and is easily accessible from all parts of the city. Tickets can be bought at booths inside the terminal or, occasionally, direct from the driver. Bus and plane tickets can also be purchased online from

the **Student Agency**. A good motorway network serves the city: D5 from the west, D1 and D2 from the southeast, D8 from the north, D11 from the east. Note that there are no toll booths; instead, a motorway usage vignette (sticker) must be fixed on the windscreen. Buy this at the border or fuel stations near it. See **Czech Motorways** for further information. Headlights must be used even during the day. In Prague, it is best to leave your vehicle in one of the guarded car parks (look for the "P+R" symbol) outside the city and use public transport.

Travelling by Metro

Operated by the **Prague Public Transit**, the underground metro system is fast, efficient, and, with a little practice, easy to navigate. There are three lines: A (green), B (yellow) and C (red). Buy tickets at newsstands or at vending machines (have coins ready) and validate them at stamping machines at the top of metro escalators. Ticket checks by inspectors are frequent and you'll pay a spot fine of Kč800 if caught travelling without a valid ticket.

By Tram

Prague's trams make it easy to see the city while saving on shoe leather. The schedules can be a bit tricky to read, however. Reroutings are frequent. Buy tickets in advance – they are available all over the city from newsagents and vending machines at metro stations. Validate your ticket by inserting it into a stamping machine on entering the tram.

By Bus

Buses serve outlying areas – they are mostly banned from the centre to ease vehicular traffic. As with the metro and trams, riders must validate their tickets by using the punching machines on the bus. For some stops, riders must notify the driver of their intention to get off by pressing a button near the door.

Tickets

Public transport tickets are valid for the metro, trams, trains, funiculars, buses and transfers within the city centre. Full price tickets (Kč32) are valid for 90 minutes; reduced priced tickets (Kč24) last 30 minutes and are usually sufficient for most trips. Children aged 6–15 pay half price. One-day (Kč110) and three-day (Kč310) passes are available and will spare you the trouble of buying individual tickets for each journey. Tickets can be purchased from newsagents as well as from vending machines installed at metro stations and some tram stops.

By Taxi

Walking or taking the metro is often a better option for getting around the city centre but taxis are relatively cheap and convenient for moderate to long hauls. Fares start at Kč40 and rise by Kč20 per kilometre. Most short journeys will cost you less than Kč200. Never hail a taxi on the street due to the risk of getting a rogue driver. Instead phone a reputable radio taxi, such as **Modrý Anděl**, **AAA Taxi** or **CityTaxi**, or book on their website.

By Car

Prague's city centre was not designed for the volume of traffic it sees now. The streets are narrow and winding and parking is scarce. If you do decide to drive, keep right, wear a seatbelt and be aware that traffic violation fines are payable on the spot. Illegally parked cars are clamped or towed away by vigilant traffic wardens.

By Bicycle

While there are numerous bicycle routes, cyclists do not usually have their own lanes and must share the road with cars, which can prove hazardous. The cobblestones can also be hard going. **Praha Bike** and **Biko Adventures** (see p138) rent out bikes and offer cycling tours.

On Foot

Walking is the best – and often the only – way to see much of the city. The centre is only about 4 km (2.5 miles) from end to end and many of the historic sights are in pedestrian zones. Make sure you wear flat-soled comfortable shoes, watch your step on the cobblestones, and keep a look out for trams that have priority of crossing even over pedestrians.

DIRECTORY

ARRIVING BY AIR

Czech Airlines
(239 007007
w csa.cz

Delta
w delta.com

EasyJet
w easyjet.com

Ryanair
w ryanair.com

Smartwings
w smartwings.com

Václav Havel Airport Prague
(220 111888
w prg.aero

Wizz Air
w wizzair.com

ARRIVING BY RAIL

Prague Main Station
(840 112113
w cd.cz

ARRIVING BY ROAD

Czech Motorways
w motorway.cz

Eurolines
w eurolines.com

Flixbus
w flixbus.com

Florenc Bus Terminal
(900 144444
w florenc.cz

Student Agency
w studentagency.eu

TRAVELLING BY METRO

Prague Public Transit
(296 191817
w dpp.cz

BY TAXI

AAA Taxi
(222 333222
w aaataxi.cz

CityTaxi
(257 257257
w citytaxi.cz/en

Modrý Anděl
(737 222333
w modryandel.cz

Practical Information

Passports and Visas

Visitors from outside the European Economic Area (EEA), European Union (EU) and Switzerland need a valid passport to enter the Czech Republic. EEA, EU and Swiss nationals can use their national identity cards instead. Citizens of Australia, New Zealand, Canada and the US can visit the Czech Republic for up to 90 days without a visa. For longer stays, a visa should be obtained from the Czech Embassy in advance. Schengen visas are valid for the Czech Republic. Most other non-EU nationals need a visa, and should consult the **Czech Ministry of Foreign Affairs** website.

Several countries, including **Australia**, **Canada**, **New Zealand**, the **UK** and the **USA**, have embassies in Prague.

Customs and Immigration

For EU citizens there are no duties on reasonable quantities of most goods meant for personal use carried in or out of the Czech Republic. Exceptions include firearms and weapons, certain types of food and plants and endangered species. Passengers from non-EU nations can import 200 cigarettes or 250 g (9 oz) of tobacco products, a litre of spirits and four litres of wine. Non-EU residents can also claim back VAT on purchases over Kč2,000 when leaving the EU *(see p138)*. If you

take regular medicine, bring adequate supplies and carry your prescription with you.

Travel Safety Advice

Visitors can get up-to-date travel safety information from the **Department of Foreign Affairs and Trade** in Australia, the **Foreign and Commonwealth Office** in the UK and the **State Department** in the US.

Travel Insurance

It is advisable to take out insurance against illness, accidents, theft or loss and travel cancellations, curtailment or delays. The Czech Republic has reciprocal health agreements with other EU countries; EU residents will receive state-provided emergency treatment if they have a valid European Health Insurance Card (EHIC) with them, but note that dental care is not covered. Non-EU visitors should check if their country has reciprocal arrangements with the Czech Republic.

Emergencies

The ambulance, police and fire brigade can be reached on the Europe-wide **emergency** number 112. The operators speak English and calls are free. There are also dedicated lines for the **ambulance**, **fire brigade** and **police**.

Health

There are no vaccinations required for visiting the Czech Republic. Tap water

is generally safe, although bottled water is widely available. There are several hospitals in Prague with 24-hour emergency rooms. A reliable central hospital accustomed to dealing with English-speaking patients is **Na Homolce Hospital**. The **Canadian Medical Centre** is a recommended private clinic. If you need emergency medical services, remember to take your passport. It's also a good idea to carry cash or a credit or debit card, as you may be required to pay in advance for some services.

For even such common medicines as aspirin or cold remedies, you'll need to visit a pharmacy, or *lékárna*. These are dotted across town and are easily identified by a large green cross. Most operate during normal working hours, from 8am to 6pm Monday to Friday, although many pharmacies in shopping centres are open on weekends. There are a handful of specialized **24-hour pharmacies**.

Czech dental care is considered to be among the best in Europe. For emergencies, call the 24/7 **Dental Emergency (Zubní pohotovost)**. For routine care, try the English-speaking dentists at **Millennium Dental Care** or **Elite Dental Prague**.

Personal Security

Prague, like all major cities, has its share of pickpockets and petty thieves who operate in crowded and congested areas like the metro and trams. Avoid flashing cash or expensive items in public. Violent crime is relatively rare, although solo travellers should still exercise sensible precautions. Avoid hailing taxis on the street; instead, call or ask someone to call for a reliable radio taxi (see p133). Report thefts to the police, especially if you need to make an insurance claim. There are several **police stations** in the centre; Jungmannovo náměstí 9 is a reliable one and is used to dealing with foreign visitors.

Lost items are normally sent to the city **Lost Property Office**.

Travellers with Specific Needs

Prague isn't the most accessible capital, but it is improving year by year. Many metro stations, especially the newer ones in outlying areas, have auditory beacons for the blind and lifts, although older stations in the centre are still inaccessible. Many trams and buses have specially lowered floors; visit the web-

site of **Prague Public Transit** (see p133) for more information. The **Prague Organization of Wheelchair Users** lobbies for the disabled. It offers a useful free brochure called Overcoming Barriers; this lists barrier-free galleries, monuments, restaurants, public toilets and shops, and has easy-to-read maps. Get the brochure and advice about disability issues at their office near Náměstí Republiky. **Accessible Prague** and **Czech Blind United** are other helpful organizations to contact.

DIRECTORY

PASSPORTS AND VISAS

Czech Ministry of Foreign Affairs
224 181111 ■ mzv.cz

Australia
MAP G2 ■ Klimentská 10, 6th floor
221 729260
■ poland.embassy.gov.au/wsaw/home.html

Canada
Ve Struhách 2
272 101800
■ canadainternational.gc.ca/czech-tcheque

UK
MAP C2 ■ Thunovská 14
257 402111
■ ukinczechrepublic.fco.gov.uk

USA
MAP C3 ■ Tržiště 15
257 022000
■ cz.usembassy.gov/cs

TRAVEL SAFETY ADVICE

Australia
Department of Foreign Affairs and Trade
■ dfat.gov.au
■ smartraveller.gov.au

United Kingdom
Foreign and Commonwealth Office
■ gov.uk/foreign-travel-advice

United States
US Department of State
■ travel.state.gov

EMERGENCIES

Emergency
112

Ambulance
155

Fire Brigade
150

Police
158

HEALTH

24-hour pharmacies
MAP H6 ■ Belgická 37
MAP F4 ■ Palackého 5
■ Vídeňská 800 (Thomayerova Hospital)
■ V Úvalu 84 (University Hospital Motol)

Canadian Medical Centre
Veleslavínská 1
■ cmcpraha.cz/en-US

Dental Emergency (Zubní pohotovost)
MAP F4 ■ Palackého 5

Elite Dental Prague
MAP F5 ■ Vodičkova 5
■ elitedental.cz

Millennium Dental Care
MAP G2 ■ V Celnicí 10
■ mdc.cz/en

Na Homolce Hospital
Roentgenova 2
■ homolka.cz/en-CZ

PERSONAL SECURITY

Lost Property Office
MAP K6 ■ Karolíny Světlé 5 224 235085

Police Station
MAP M6
■ Jungmannovo náměstí 9
974 851710
■ policie.cz

TRAVELLERS WITH SPECIFIC NEEDS

Accessible Prague
Moravanu 51
608 531753
■ accessibleprague.com

Czech Blind United
MAP G5 ■ Krakovská 21
221 462462
■ sons.cz

Prague Organization of Wheelchair Users
MAP N2 ■ Benediktská 6
224 826078
■ pov.cz
■ presbariery.cz

Currency and Banking

The Czech Republic's currency is the koruna or crown (Kč), divided into 100 haléřů. Notes come in denominations of Kč100, 200, 500, 1,000, 2,000 and 5,000. Coins are Kč1, 2, 5, 10, 20 and 50, and are handy for paying for transport tickets and public toilets.

Most banks have ATMs (cash machines) in a lobby or outside wall. These can be accessed by card at any time. Czech ATMs require a four-digit pin. Beware of ATM crime, and always shield your pin from view. Some banks require you to notify them of your travel plans before departure to avoid having the bank block your card for fraud protection.

Private money exchange counters (called bureaux de change) are not advisable for changing money. While they are required by law to post their rates on the window – and they all claim "zero per cent commission" – they almost always have hidden fees and higher charges than advertised. A safer option is to get Czech currency at a reputable bank, such as the **UniCredit Bank**. It is best to convert only as much cash as you will need, as it is often difficult to exchange koruna outside the country.

Prepaid currency cards (cash passports) are a more secure way of carrying money. They can be loaded with koruna, fixing exchange rates before you leave, and used like a debit card.

Major credit cards, such as Visa, MasterCard and American Express, are widely accepted and very useful in restaurants, car rentals, hotels and shops and for booking theatre or cinema tickets online.

Internet and Telephone

Internet access is easy to find in Prague. Wi-Fi is available in most hotels and in many public places such as restaurants, cafés and pubs. There are internet bars and cafés in the city but you can also surf the net at your hotel if you do not have a smartphone or laptop. Some visitors do their surfing at the **Globe Bookstore and Café** (see p120).

The Czech Republic's international telephone code is 420. There are no area codes in the country, and all phone numbers, with the exception of some emergency hotlines, are unique strings of nine digits. When calling the Czech Republic from abroad, dial your country's international access code followed by 420 and then the nine-digit number. To call abroad from Prague, dial "+" or 00 followed by the country code, then the area code and number.

To use your mobile device in the country, it will need to be equipped for GSM network frequencies 1800 MHz. If your phone doesn't have an EU SIM card, consider buying a local SIM card, available at phone shops around town. You'll get a local number and pay lower charges for calls, text and data. To use a local SIM though, your device must be unlocked. Alternatively, ask your home provider how to use the phone abroad and activate an international roaming plan to keep costs down. Without such a plan, avoid using your phone since roaming fees soar quickly – use it only when on a Wi-Fi network.

When not out of order, payphones accept either coins or phone cards (telefonní karty), which are available at post offices and newsagents.

Postal Services

The **Main Post Office** (Hlavní pošta) is lovely inside and worth a visit, whether or not you need to mail a postcard or letter overseas. It also offers a large phone room, which is a good way of making overseas telephone calls.

Television, Radio and Newspapers

If your hotel has a satellite hook-up, expect the usual fare of CNN, Sky News and MTV. **Radio Prague**, the foreign-language service of state-run Czech Radio, broadcasts news and features in English and five other languages. You can listen or read features in English on their website. The BBC broadcasts in English at 101.1 FM. There are no longer any locally published English-language papers in the country, but international publications like the *Wall Street Journal*, the *Guardian*, and the *New York Times* are available at city centre newsstands.

Opening Hours

Shops in the city centre generally work 9am–6pm

Monday to Saturday. Malls and shopping centres stay open until 8pm or 9pm. Sunday has limited trading hours. These vary but stores catering to tourists work 10am–6pm.

Major banks open at 9am and close at 5pm or 6pm on weekdays. Museums and galleries generally open 10am–6pm Tuesday to Sunday, with most closing on Mondays. Last admission to many attractions is 30 minutes before closing.

Time Difference

The Czech Republic is on Central European Time (CET), which is the same time zone as much of Western Europe. It is 11 hours behind Australian Eastern Standard Time (AEST), 6 hours ahead of US Eastern Standard Time (EST) and an hour ahead of Greenwich Mean Time (GMT). The clock moves forward 1 hour during daylight saving time (last Sunday in March until the last Sunday in October).

Electrical Appliances

The electricity supply is 220–240V AC. Plugs come with two round pins, the standard plug type used across much of Continental Europe. Depending on the appliance, you'll need an adaptor and possibly also a converter. Many modern electronics, like laptops and mobiles, have a built-in transformer and only require an adaptor.

Driving Licences

To hire a car, you must be 19 and have held a full licence for at least a year. You'll need your passport, plus your credit card for the security deposit. It is recommended that all non-EU visitors carry an International Driving Permit (IDP). While driving, you must carry your licence and the car registration and rental papers, and display the motorway vignette (see p132).

Weather

The weather in Prague is unpredictable, and given the northern European climate, an umbrella or raincoat will be handy all year around. The best times to visit are spring and autumn, without the summer crowds and with relatively reliable weather. Winter is comparatively quiet, although the benefits of having the city to yourself are offset by daytime highs just above freezing and sunsets at 5pm. Depending on the year, summer can be hot and muggy or cool and rainy. Even in midsummer it's wise to pack a sweater for the evenings.

Visitor Information

Prague City Tourism is the city's official tourist-information service. It has offices at the airport, plus three in town: on the Old Town Square, Wenceslas Square and at Na Můstku. English-speaking staff dispense brochures, maps and information on what's on, where to eat, where to stay and transport. Their official website is useful and well laid out.

The popular **Expats.cz** and **Prague.tv** carry event and film listings, articles on Prague life and restaurant reviews.

The **Taste of Prague** blog is by a Czech couple, both avowed foodies, on what to eat and where to eat it; they also run food tours. The **Living Prague** site, by a tourist turned resident, offers personal experiences and advice. **Houser** is a countercultural site with great event and festival listings. Although it's in Czech, it's not hard to navigate.

DIRECTORY

CURRENCY AND BANKING

UniCredit Bank
MAP P3 ■ Náměstí Republiky 3a
📞 955 959835
🌐 unicreditbank.cz

POSTAL SERVICES

Main Post Office
MAP P6 ■ Jindřišská 14
📞 221 131111
🌐 ceskaposta.cz

TELEVISION, RADIO AND NEWSPAPERS

Radio Prague
🌐 radio.cz

VISITOR INFORMATION

Expats.cz
🌐 expats.cz

Houser
🌐 houser.cz

Living Prague
🌐 livingprague.com

Prague City Tourism
MAP M5 ■ Rytířská 12
MAP M4 ■
Staroměstské náměstí 1
MAP G4 ■ Václavské náměstí 42
🌐 prague.eu

Prague.tv
🌐 prague.tv

Taste of Prague
🌐 tasteofprague.com

Trips and Tours

There is no shortage of fun ways to tour the city, whether on foot, by bus, bicycle, boat or in a horse-drawn carriage.

Guided walking tours abound, with themes that include historic Prague, Communist Prague, and haunted Prague. Most tours meet up just below the Astronomical Clock on Old Town Square. Markéta Hradecká from **Caput Regni Private Tours** is a respected private guide. **Wittman Tours** focuses on Jewish heritage and offers highly regarded walking tours of the city's former Jewish quarter, plus bus tours to the former Nazi concentration camp at Terezín, north of Prague.

Established bus tour companies **Martin Tour** and **Premiant** offer a menu of outings from a few hours to a whole day.

Filippo Mari at **Biko Adventures** offers mountain-bike tours of Prague and its environs and rents out bikes. **Praha Bike** also rent out bicycles and run guided city bike tours.

Several operators, such as **Prague Venice**, run boat tours down the Vltava in summer. The boats generally set off from Charles, Palackého and Čechův bridges.

For the romantics, horse-drawn carriages wait at the Old Town Square. Segways were banned from the Old Town in 2016, but **Prague on Segway** still run tours to other parts of the city.

Shopping

Prague is an underrated shopping destination and some of the best shopping areas have been picked out in this guide. Designer labels such as **Prada** and **Hermès**, congregate along the cobblestoned Pařížská street, which runs north of Old Town Square. The area around Wenceslas Square and Na Příkopě is home to names with more affordable high-street appeal like **Zara**. It's also where you'll find the city's biggest and best shopping mall, **Palladium**.

The bigger museums, galleries and tourist sites usually have gift stores with books, posters, postcards and T-shirts.

The city is a paradise for antique hunters, and the centre has several junk merchants and antique shops. Keep an eye out for the words *starožitnosti* or *antik* somewhere on the outside. Objects to look for include 19th and early 20th-century household articles, glassware, textiles and furnishings. An *antikvariát* is similar, but usually specializing in old books. These can be terrific places for old posters, maps and paintings.

The central streets in Malá Strana and the Old Town are dominated by souvenir shops, but very few of these flashy stores, hawking cheap trinkets, "Prague Drinking Team" sweatshirts and KGB hats, are selling anything of real value. Instead look for authentic high-quality glass with eye-catching classical designs at **Moser** (see p88) or find deep-red Czech garnets at the three **Granát** stores in Prague.

Most of the larger shops will accept leading credit cards. VAT (Value Added Tax) is charged at 21 per cent and is almost always included in the marked price of the item. Some stores offer tax-free shopping for non-EU residents and will display a sign and provide a Global Refund form for customs to validate at the airport when you leave the EU (see p134).

Dining

Diners have a wealth of choice in the centre. In addition to the restaurants and pubs serving typical Czech dishes such as roast pork and duck, there are now dozens of places where you can find decent Italian, Indian, Mexican and other cuisines.

Meat- and dairy-free dining is no longer the problem it was a few years ago. Many popular restaurants offer vegetarians a wide variety of meatless meals. These include the **Lehká Hlava** restaurant (see p91) in the Old Town, the **Country Life** organic health-food shops and vegan cafés across town, the **Malý Buddha** Vietnamese restaurant (see p105) in Hradčany and the **Dhaba Beas** north Indian vegan self-service cafés in eight locations across the city. Older establishments are also increasingly sensitive to vegetarians' needs.

Praguers generally have dinner from 7pm to 9pm and lunch from 11am to 2pm or 3pm, when pubs, cafés, and fast-food restaurants fill up. This can be a good time to frequent the more expensive restaurants, which seek to attract the lunchtime crowds by offering cheaper set menus, called a *denní menu* or *polední nabídka*. Czechs rarely eat breakfast out, so it's a good idea to eat at your hotel's breakfast buffet before heading off sightseeing in the morning.

There are several online sites in English offering reviews of the latest restaurants and dining trends. **Expats.cz** *(see p137)* publishes helpful feature articles written by locals. **Taste of Prague** *(see p137)* and **Bohemian Bites** are popular and informative foodie blogs.

Tipping in Prague is a straightforward affair. Simply round up the bill to the nearest 50 or 100Kč. Leave the money on the table or give it directly to the server. It is always a good idea to reserve a table in advance, since the better places tend to fill up fast every night.

Where to Stay

The better properties in desirable parts of Prague, such as the Old Town, Hradčany and Malá Strana, can be pricey, but with so much choice, it generally pays to shop around, especially online. Visitors can save a considerable amount on their hotel bill by exploring accommodation options outside the central areas. The neighbourhoods of Žižkov, Karlín, Smíchov and Holešovice, for example, all have good connections to the centre and an increasing number of good-quality hotels.

As well as hotels for every budget, there are self-catering apartments, B&Bs, private homes and hostels for rent. Budget hotel chains often offer double rooms in good locations for as little as €69 per night. Room-finding services like **Mary's** offer accommodation for every budget. **AirBnB** has an active Prague section offering everything from luxurious home stays to flopping on someone's couch.

For short-term apartment rentals ideal for families and groups, **Prague-stay. com** has a hard-to-beat list of gorgeous flats at reasonable prices. Many Prague hotels list with the **Booking.com** site, which has a clean, easy-to-use web interface.

Hotels in Prague usually quote room rates, rather than prices per person, and include VAT in their published rates. The rates will generally, although not always, include breakfast. The best price deals at budget hotel chains are to be had well in advance and online.

The peak tourist season in Prague runs roughly from April to May and September to October, with high prices in peak seasons. Prices are slightly lower from June to August, which is crowded but considered shoulder season. The lowest prices are to be found between November and March, outside the holiday period.

DIRECTORY

TRIPS AND TOURS

Biko Adventures
w bikoadventures.com

Caput Regni Private Tours
w caputregni.cz

Martin Tour
w martintour.cz

Prague on Segway
w pragueonsegway.com

Prague Venice
w prague-venice.cz

Praha Bike
w prahabike.cz

Premiant
w premiant.cz

Wittman Tours
w wittmann-tours.com

SHOPPING

Granát
w granat.eu

Hermès
MAP L3 ∎ Pařížská 12
w hermes.com

Moser
MAP N5 ∎ Na Příkopě 12
w moser-glass.com

Palladium
MAP P3 ∎ Náměstí Republiky 1
w palladiumpraha.cz

Prada
MAP L2 ∎ Pařížská 16
w prada.com

Zara
MAP N5 ∎ Na Příkopě 15
w zara.com

DINING

Bohemian Bites
w bohemianbites.
wordpress.com

Country Life
w countrylife.cz

Dhaba Beas
w beas-dhaba.cz

WHERE TO STAY

Airbnb
w airbnb.com

Booking.com
w booking.com

Mary's
w marys.cz

Prague-stay.com
w prague-stay.com

Places to Stay

PRICE CATEGORIES
For a standard, double room per night (with breakfast if included), taxes and extra charges.

Ⓚ under Kč3,000 ⠀⠀ ⓀⓀ Kč3,000–6,000
ⓀⓀⓀ over Kč6,000

Luxury Hotels

Archibald At the Charles Bridge
MAP D3 ▪ Na Kampě 15 ▪ 234 652800 ▪ www.archibald.cz ▪ ⓀⓀ
Also known by its address Na Kampě 15, the hotel "At the Charles Bridge" is close enough to the river that guests can hear the Vltava rushing over the weir and the cries of the gulls. The rooms and suites are warmly furnished in a country style.

Hotel Hoffmeister
MAP D1 ▪ Pod Bruskou 7 ▪ 251 017111 ▪ www.hoffmeister.cz ▪ ⓀⓀ
The Hoffmeister is a quiet, modern hotel in the shadow of Prague Castle, celebrated for its gourmet restaurant and gallery of caricatures by the owner's father. The airy rooms are sumptuously and uniquely furnished, and there are lovely outdoor spaces. There is an excellent spa.

Hotel Pod věží
MAP D3 ▪ Mostecká 2 ▪ 257 532041 ▪ www.podvezi.com ▪ ⓀⓀ
The "Hotel Under the Tower" guards the Malá Strana end of Charles Bridge. Rooms are graciously outfitted with period furniture and comfortable reproductions. Hairstylists, barbers, manicurists and masseuses are on call.

Hotel U krále Karla
MAP B2 ▪ Úvoz 4 ▪ 257 531211 ▪ www.ukralekarla.cz ▪ ⓀⓀ
The two town houses in which the King Charles Hotel is set were created in 1639 from a Gothic Benedictine building. The hotel was popular in the 17th century for the healing powers of its well. The decor is a blissful marriage of Baroque furnishings and modern luxuries.

Four Seasons
MAP K3 ▪ Veleslavínova 2a ▪ 221 427000 ▪ www.fourseasons.com ▪ ⓀⓀⓀ
Swaddled in the classic Four Seasons trademark luxury, guests may well forget where they are. A quick stroll on the hotel's riverside terrace should remind them. The Cotto-Crudo restaurant is among Prague's best.

Grand Hotel Bohemia
MAP P3 ▪ Králodvorská 4 ▪ 234 608111 ▪ www.grandhotelbohemia.cz ▪ ⓀⓀⓀ
Old European decorum meets Old European decadence: built in 1920, the Bohemia was home to one of the liveliest clubs in Jazz Age Prague. Its 79 rooms were refurbished in 2002 with elegant dark wood and cream furnishings. The best views are from the eighth floor.

Hotel Paříž
MAP P3 ▪ U Obecního domu 1 ▪ 222 195666 ▪ www.hotel-pariz.cz ▪ ⓀⓀⓀ
Built in 1904, this Art Nouveau treasure with its stunning staircase retains all its original charm while incorporating modern conveniences such as heated bathroom floors and king-size beds in all rooms. The Royal Tower Suite has a spectacular 360° view.

Mandarin Oriental
MAP C3 ▪ Nebovidská 1 ▪ 233 088888 ▪ www.mandarinoriental.com/prague ▪ ⓀⓀⓀ
The hotel is located in a restored Dominican monastery. Its spa is in the former chapel and several of its 99 rooms have views over the city to Prague Castle.

The Mark
MAP G3 ▪ Hybernská 12 ▪ 226 226111 ▪ www.mprague.cz ▪ ⓀⓀⓀ
Once the Baroque Palace U Věžníků, The Mark offers an appealing blend of the historical and the contemporary. The rooms and suites are comfortable. Amenities include a spa and wellness centre, as well as conference rooms. There is a gorgeous garden and terrace open all summer for dining.

Radisson Blu Alcron
MAP G4 ▪ Štepánská 40 ▪ 222 820000 ▪ radissonblu.com/hotel-prague ▪ ⓀⓀⓀ
In the 1930s the Alcron was Prague's answer to the Ritz in New York.

This historic hotel with period furnishings and high ceilings has had its Art Nouveau dandiness – besmirched by 40 years of secret police surveillance – revived by the Radisson group. Try the Be Bop bar or La Rotonde restaurant, or the Michelin-starred Alcron restaurant (see p71), which boasts one of the country's top chefs, Roman Paulus.

Smetana Hotel

MAP K6 ▪ Karoliny Světlé 34 ▪ 234 705111 ▪ www. smetanahotel.com ▪ ⓚⓚⓚ

Located on the waterfront, the Smetana offers spectacular views. Rooms are luxuriously over the top, with frescoes, chapel ceilings, architectural gems and medieval decor, fittings and fixtures. It is so romantic that it may be hard to leave your room.

U Zlaté studně

MAP C2 ▪ U Zlaté studně 4 ▪ 257 011213 ▪ www. goldenwell.cz ▪ ⓚⓚⓚ

Once belonging to the astronomer Tycho Brahe, "At the Golden Well" sits in Malá Strana's twisting maze of streets, adjoining the Ledeburg Gardens and offering unparalleled views. Rooms have whirlpool baths and Richelieu furniture. The terrace restaurant is one of Prague's top choices (see p71).

Old Town Hotels

Hotel Aurus

MAP K5 ▪ Karlova 3 ▪ 222 220262 ▪ www.aurus hotel.cz ▪ ⓚⓚ

You'll tell the folks back home about this one. Set in the heart of Prague, this family-run four-star property is a beautiful historical monument protected by UNESCO. Exuding old-world charm, rooms are distinctive and have antique furnishings. Charles Bridge and the Old Town Square are only a short walk away.

Hotel Clementin

MAP K4 ▪ Seminářská 4 ▪ 222 231520 ▪ www. clementin.cz ▪ ⓚⓚ

The Clementin has the honour of being Prague's narrowest preserved building. As you might expect, the nine rooms in this Gothic edifice are small, but pleasant. You might struggle with large luggage.

Hotel Cloister Inn

MAP K6 ▪ Konviktská 14 ▪ 224 211020 ▪ www. cloister-inn.com ▪ ⓚⓚ

The Jesuits founded the cloister, in 1660, that gives the hotel its name. It was then home to the Grey Sisters of St Francis, who were displaced by the secret police. The complex was returned to them in 1990. All 75 rooms have modern amenities.

Hotel Josef

MAP N2 ▪ Rybná 20 ▪ 221 700111 ▪ www. hoteljosef.com ▪ ⓚⓚ

Modern and trendy, this designer hotel fits in with Prague's urban chic image with its simple, clean-cut white and glass interiors and spacious rooms. Two buildings are connected by a courtyard, offering unique design elements. The lobby is a showpiece in itself. There is a stylish hotel bar, plus a fitness room and sauna. Sign up for a morning sightseeing jog.

Hotel Metamorphis

MAP N3 ▪ Malá Štupartská 5 ▪ 221 771011 ▪ www.meta morphis.cz ▪ ⓚⓚ

Stylish touches, including parquet floors and tiled stoves, and stirring views of the Ungelt courtyard and St James set this place apart. The patio restaurant does big business in the summer. No lift.

Hotel U staré paní

MAP L5 ▪ Michalská 9 ▪ 222 539539 ▪ No air conditioning ▪ www.hotel ustarepani.cz ▪ ⓚⓚ

A no-frills modern affair, staffed with an amiable crew. All 17 rooms have a minibar and satellite TV, but for better entertainment, catch the acts at the club below (see p89).

Hotel Ungelt

MAP N3 ▪ Štupartská 7 ▪ 221 771011 ▪ No air conditioning ▪ www. ungelt.cz ▪ ⓚⓚ

The immediate vicinity is said to be haunted by at least two ghosts, but guests at the Ungelt have registered no complaints. Perhaps they're sleeping far too soundly in one of the nine renovated 10th-century apartments to notice. The courtyard offers glimpses of Týn Church. Book early.

Lippert

MAP M3 ▪ Mikulášská 2 ▪ 224 232250 ▪ www. lipperthotel.cz ▪ ⓚⓚ

Across the street from Franz Kafka's birthplace, with views of St Nicholas and Týn churches, the Black Fox building is listed as a UNESCO World Cultural Heritage Site. There are only 12 rooms, so book well in advance.

U Medvídků
MAP L6 ▪ Na Perštýně 7
▪ No air conditioning
▪ www.umedvidku.cz
▪ ⓀⓀ

Not only is "At the Small Bears" centrally located, it is also close to tram and metro stations. Connected to a historic brewery, it is set above the city's favourite Budvar pub. The rooms are charming, with Gothic rafters and Renaissance painted ceilings.

Casa Marcello
MAP N1 ▪ Řásnovka 783 ▪ 222 311230 ▪ www.casa-marcello.cz ▪ ⓀⓀⓀ
The elegantly appointed rooms embrace their 13th-century character. Wandering through the stairs and hallways, you might think you're in an Escher print. There is a small fitness club and excellent restaurant.

Intercontinental
MAP E1 ▪ Pařížská 30
▪ 296 631111 ▪ www.ihg.com ▪ ⓀⓀⓀⓀ
The Intercontinental pulls out all the stops for its Club Level guests, but all its guests will feel pampered. The large fitness centre has a swimming pool, exercise machines and a spa. Rooms with city views are less expensive than those that overlook the Vltava.

Malá Strana and Hradčany Hotels

Biskupský dům
MAP D3 ▪ Dražického náměstí 6 ▪ 257 532320
▪ No air conditioning
▪ www.hotelbishops house.cz ▪ ⓀⓀ
The Bishop's House hotel actually occupies two

buildings: one is the former residence of the bishop of Prague; the other was a butcher's in the 18th century. Between them are 45 rooms, all of which are comfortable and tastefully furnished.

Domus Henrici
MAP B2 ▪ Loretánská 11
▪ 220 511369 ▪ No air conditioning ▪ www.domus-henrici.cz ▪ ⓀⓀ
Built in 1372 on the steep hill overlooking the city, this small hotel is a stone's throw from the castle. All eight rooms have views of Petřín Hill and thoughtful amenities such as rocking chairs.

Dům U Červeného Lva
MAP C2 ▪ Nerudova 41
▪ 257 533832 ▪ No air conditioning ▪ www.hotelredlion.cz ▪ ⓀⓀ
From the hotel "At the Red Lion", guests can see either Prague Castle and Nerudova to the north or Petřín Hill to the south. Guests will find it hard to leave room No. 32.

Hotel Čertovka
MAP D2 ▪ U lužického semináře 2 ▪ 257 011500
▪ www.certovka.cz
▪ ⓀⓀ
You can watch boats pass beneath Charles Bridge on the Čertovka canal from windows overlooking Prague's "Little Venice". Top-floor rooms have views of Prague castle. Parking is some distance from the hotel, however.

Hotel Sax
MAP B3 ▪ Jánský vršek 3
▪ 257 531268 ▪ www.sax.cz ▪ ⓀⓀ
Tucked into the heart of Malá Strana, the modern

Sax is close to the Church of Our Lady Victorious, St Nicholas's Church, and Prague Castle. Decked out in 1950s, 1960s and 1970s style, the 19 colourful rooms and three suites arranged around a bright central atrium are simple yet cosy.

Hotel Waldstein
MAP C2 ▪ Valdštejnske náměstí 6 ▪ 257 533938
▪ No air conditioning
▪ www.hotelwaldstein.cz
▪ ⓀⓀ
Adjoining Duke Albrecht von Wallenstein's palace on a quiet courtyard, this cosy hotel features 15 rooms and ten suites. All the rooms are very comfortable and are furnished with a variety of antiques and reproductions.

Rezidence Lundborg
MAP D2 ▪ U lužického semináře 3 ▪ 257 011911
▪ www.lundborg.se ▪ ⓀⓀ
In case the view of the Charles Bridge isn't enough, each of the 13 suites in this 700-year-old building is equipped with a Jacuzzi and a computer with free internet access. In the cellar, you'll find remnants of the foundations of the 12th-century Judith Bridge, destroyed by floods in 1342.

U Tří Pštrosů
MAP D3 ▪ Dražického náměstí 12 ▪ 777 876667
▪ No air conditioning
▪ www.utripstrosu.cz
▪ ⓀⓀ
"At the Three Ostriches" gets its name from a 16th-century owner who was a purveyor of ostrich feathers. The rooms are comfortable and very quiet given their proximity to Charles Bridge.

Zlatá Hvězda

MAP C2 ■ Nerudova 48
■ 257 532867 ■ No air
conditioning ■ www.
hotelgoldenstar.cz ■ ⓀⓀ
Built as the residence of
Hradčany's mayor in 1372,
the Golden Star has a
long history of elegance.
The apartments and
rooms have period furni-
ture and modern baths.
Room No. 33 is sublime.

Aria

MAP C3 ■ Tržiště 9 ■ 225
334111 ■ www.ariahotel.
net ■ ⓀⓀⓀ
An unusual little hotel,
where each of the themed
rooms, though not large,
is dedicated to a musical
legend, be it Mozart or
Dizzy Gillespie. The hotel's
musical director will also
advise you on concerts
you can attend. Guests
have private access to the
garden at Prague Castle.

Augustine

MAP D2 ■ Letenská 12/33 ■
266 112233 ■ www.augus
tinehotel.com ■ ⓀⓀⓀ
Sited in the 13th-century
Augustinian monastery of
St Thomas, this luxury
hotel offers rooms and
suites (some created by
combining the monks'
cells) with Cubist-style
furnishings popular in
Prague in the 1920s and
1930s. There is a bar set
in the cellar of the original
St Thomas Brewery.

New Town Hotels

Novoměstský Hotel

MAP F5 ■ Řeznická 4
■ 221 419911 ■ No air
conditioning ■ www.
novomestskyhotel.cz ■ Ⓚ
A bit old-fashioned, but
the staff are helpful.
Close to Karlovo náměstí
and the New Town Hall.

Hotel 16 U Sv. Kateřiny

MAP F6 ■ Kateřinská 16
■ 224 919676 ■ www.
hotel16.cz ■ ⓀⓀ
The apartments and rooms
at the luxuriously furnished
St Catherine's are great
value. Set near the river
and the Prague Botanical
Gardens, this family-run
inn is quiet, with charming
eccentricities like the
display of lovely junk from
the next-door bazaar.

Hotel Grandium

MAP P6 ■ Politických
vězňů 12 ■ 234 100100
■ www.hotel-grandium.
cz ■ ⓀⓀ
Designed with luxury in
mind, the 196 rooms have
fresh, contemporary
decor. The hotel's sum-
mer terrace and the light
airy feel provide a distinct
difference from other
offerings in the area.

Hotel Icon

MAP F4 ■ V jámě 6 ■ 221
634100 ■ www.iconhotel.
eu ■ ⓀⓀ
This hip boutique hotel
has natural handmade
beds from Sweden. An
all day breakfast, docks
for smartphones in each
room, complimentary
Rituals toiletries and a
massage centre are just
some of the extras.

Hotel Jalta

MAP N6 ■ Václavské
náměstí 45 ■ 222 822111
■ www.hoteljalta.cz
■ ⓀⓀ
This Wenceslas Square
designer hotel offers 89
stylish rooms and five
luxurious suites. The
Como restaurant serves
excellent Mediterranean
cuisine. There is also a
casino, a fitness centre
and a business centre.

Hotel Jungmann

MAP M6 ■ Jungmannovo
náměstí 2 ■ 224 219501
■ www.antikhotels.com
■ ⓀⓀ
This charming hotel is
situated in one of the
narrowest houses in
Prague near Wenceslas
Square and other sights
of interest. It has 12 en-
suite double rooms, each
with Wi-Fi and air condi-
tioning. Parking arranged
on request at the nearby
National Theatre.

Hotel Opera

MAP H1 ■ Těšnov 13
■ 222 315609 ■ www.
hotel-opera.cz ■ ⓀⓀ
The rooms at the Hotel
Opera are more low-key
than its rosy pink Neo-
Renaissance façade
suggests. They are great
value for money, bright
and comfortable.

Majestic Plaza

MAP F5 ■ Štěpánská 33
■ 221 486100 ■ www.
hotel-majestic.cz ■ ⓀⓀ
This popular hotel is set
in two interconnected
buildings, one of which
was where writer Jaroslav
Hašek (see p44) was born.
Art Deco and Biedermeier-
style rooms are on offer,
along with great views
from the seventh floor.

Art Deco Imperial Hotel

MAP G2 ■ Na Poříčí 15 ■
246 011600 ■ www.hotel-
imperial.cz ■ ⓀⓀⓀ
This hotel is aimed at
leisure and business
travellers who prefer
the intimacy and
individual approach of
a boutique hotel. Modern
technology and comforts
combine seamlessly
with the original Art
Deco interiors.

For a key to hotel price categories *see p140*

Boscolo Prague

MAP G3 ▪ Senovážné námeští 13 ▪ 224 593111 ▪ prague.boscolohotels.com ▪ Ⓚ Ⓚ Ⓚ

Close to the main train station, this elegant hotel boasts Italian opulence, efficient staff and an impressive spa. Make sure you opt for the breakfast package – it is well worth the extra cost.

Hotel Adria

MAP N6 ▪ Václavské námeští 26 ▪ 221 081111 ▪ www.adria.cz ▪ Ⓚ Ⓚ Ⓚ

Carmelite nuns serving at the Church of Our Lady of the Snows had their convent here in the 14th century. The 89 snug rooms look out either on the pretty Franciscan Gardens or busy Wenceslas Square. Guarded parking nearby.

Hotel Palace

MAP N5 ▪ Panská 12 ▪ 224 093111 ▪ www.palacehotel.cz ▪ Ⓚ Ⓚ Ⓚ

As classy as the hotels around the corner on Wenceslas Square, the Art Nouveau hotel is renowned for its excellent service. It offers several packages, including a two-day honeymoon deal, complete with tours and other extras. Little luxuries include marble-lined bathrooms.

Hostels

Boathouse Hostel

Lodnická 1 ▪ 603 436102 ▪ No air conditioning ▪ No credit cards ▪ www.hostelboathouse.com ▪ Ⓚ

Located 20 minutes south of the centre and run according to strict rules, the Boathouse is not a

party hostel. Laundry, bicycle and boat rental are available. There are three to nine beds to a room.

Chili Hostel

MAP E5 ▪ Pštrossova 7/205 ▪ 603 119113 ▪ www.chili.dj ▪ Ⓚ

Located near the Vltava and the National Theatre, Chili provides rooms for solo backpackers, large tour groups, schools, families and couples. It has a fully equipped kitchen, free internet and a basement party room.

Hostel Advantage

MAP G5 ▪ Sokolská 11 ▪ 224 914062 ▪ No air conditioning ▪ www.advantagehostel.cz ▪ Ⓚ

Accommodation ranges from singles to nine-bed rooms. Kitchenette and TV, free Wi-Fi and two PCs are close to the reception desk.

Hostel ELF

MAP H3 ▪ Husitská 11 ▪ 222 540963 ▪ No air conditioning ▪ www.hostelelf.com ▪ Ⓚ

On the second floor of a *fin de siècle* building near the main bus and train stations, Hostel ELF's rooms range from singles to 12-bed dorms. There is a garden, shared kitchen and common room. The staff will arrange walking tours for you.

Hostel Sokol

MAP D3 ▪ Nosticova 2a ▪ 222 540963 ▪ No air conditioning ▪ www.hostelsokol.cz ▪ Ⓚ

This central Malá Strana hostel takes its name from a First Republic national fitness movement. The six doubles and eight 12-bed

rooms are at the top of a challenging set of stairs. No smoking.

Hostel Strahov

MAP A4 ▪ Vaníčkova 7, Strahov ▪ 234 678111 ▪ No air conditioning ▪ recepce@suz.cvut.cz

The dorms provide student housing through the school year, although Block 12 is always open.

Miss Sophie's

MAP G6 ▪ Melounova 2 ▪ 246 032621 ▪ www.sophieshostel.com ▪ Ⓚ

Located not far from the centre, this is an ideal base from which to explore the city. It offers dorms as well as private rooms with en-suite bathrooms. Slightly more expensive are the apartments, which come complete with a kitchen.

Old Prague Hostel

MAP N2 ▪ Benediktská 2 ▪ 224 829058 ▪ No air conditioning ▪ www.oldpraguehostel.com ▪ Ⓚ

In central Prague, this hostel has two- to five-bed rooms and four- to eight-bed dorms, some with private showers. There's a fully equipped kitchen and dining room, movie lounge and free internet access.

Sir Toby's Hostel

MAP B5 ▪ Dělnická 24, Holešovice ▪ 246 032611 ▪ No air conditioning ▪ www.sirtobys.com ▪ Ⓚ

The staff here go to great lengths to be hospitable, throwing the occasional barbecue and helping travellers find other accommodation when Sir

Toby's is full. The baths, bedrooms and kitchen are immaculately clean.

Travellers' Hostel
MAP M2 ■ Dlouhá 33
■ 777 738608 ■ No air conditioning ■ www. travellers.cz ■ Ⓚ
This company has more than 25 years' experience hosting wanderers in a network of hostels. This Old Town hostel is above the Roxy club (see p68), but keep your carousing to a minimum, since you share the building with anxious neighbours. Other locations are open during the summer.

Pensions and B&Bs

Čelakovskeho sady
MAP G5 ■ Čelakovského sady 8 ■ 233 920118
■ No air conditioning
■ Ⓚ
Overlooking the small green surrounding the National Museum, this wonderful B&B is located just a three-minute walk from Wenceslas Square. The homely apartments and rooms are fully furnished, right down to the pots and pans in the kitchen, and the owners are very friendly.

Church Pension
MAP M6 ■Jungmannova 9 ■ 603 554785 or 296 245432 ■ No air condi-tioning ■ www.church pension.cz ■ Ⓚ
The Evangelic Church of the Czech Brethren has put its hospitality skills to the test at this small guesthouse. The rooms are suitably austere and not all have en-suite bathrooms. As this is a Christian guesthouse, you may encounter a

prayer group in the common room. The hosts are pleasant people.

Hotel and Residence Standard
MAP B6 ■ Rašínovo nábřeží 38 ■ 224 916060
■ www.standard.cz ■ Ⓚ
First-rate accommodation in a Jugendstil house along the Vltava, with nine double rooms and two suites. Guests have the use of a private garage. Children under seven stay for free.

Pension Cora
Ve Studeném 7a, Braník
■ 733 226342 ■ No air conditioning ■ www. corahotel.cz ■ Ⓚ
Located in a peaceful villa quarter in southern Prague, the Cora is not central, but nearby buses and the pension's cars can take you anywhere you need to go. Amenities include satellite TV and a billiard room. The hosts serve a big breakfast.

Pension Dientzenhofer
MAP D3 ■ Nosticova 2
■ 257 311319 ■ www. dientzenhofer.cz ■ Ⓚ
This quiet house on the banks of the Čertovka canal is the birthplace of architect Kilian Ignaz Dientzenhofer, who built the nearby Church of St Nicholas and other Baroque edifices. This famous pension boasts shabby-chic rooms and an idyllic garden with river views.

Pension Kliská
MAP B5 ■ Veltěžská 26
■ 284 687289 ■ www. pensionkliska.cz ■ Ⓚ
This small guesthouse is situated in a quiet

residential suburb of the city. The nearest metro station, Kobylisy (Line C), is a mere 5-minute walk away. From there, it is only five stops to bustling Wenceslas Square in the heart of town.

Pension Vyšehrad
MAP B6 ■ Krokova 6
■ 241 408455
■ No air conditioning
■ www.pension-vysehrad.cz ■ Ⓚ
This lovely guesthouse is nearly inside the Vyšehrad walls. Stroll through the park each evening at sunset or sit in the pension's stunning garden. The five rooms are simply and comfortably furnished. Good access to public transport. Pets stay free.

Residence Liliová
MAP K5 ■ Liliová 18
■ 226 808200
■ No air conditioning
■ www.hotelliliova prague.com ■ Ⓚ
Located just around the corner from Charles Bridge, this lovely guesthouse in a historic Prague building provides visitors with a quiet and comfortable place to stay.

Royal Boutique Residence
MAP K5 ■ Řetězová 3
■ 773 658752
■ www.pragueresidences. com ■ Ⓚ
This hotel is housed in the oldest building, a 12th-century Roman palace that was home to Jiří z Poděbrad (King George) in the 15th century. There are eight large and fully furnished, luxury apartments.

For a key to hotel price categories see p140

U Raka

MAP A2 ■ Černínská 10 ■ 220 511100 ■ www. hoteluraka.cz ■ ⓚⓚ
Prague's most romantic address, "At the Crayfish" started out as a barn in 1739. Inside its log walls today are some charming country-style rooms. Room No. 6 has its own garden, fireplace and well. Located near Prague Castle and the Loreto. Children over the age of 12 are welcome.

Apartments

Apartment Jiřího z Poděbrad

MAP B6 ■ Náměstí Jiřího z Poděbrad 6, Praha 3 – Žižkov ■ 775 588511 ■ No air conditioning ■ www.apartments-in-prague.org ■ ⓚ
This one-bedroom, spacious flat on a tree-lined Vinohradská street near a metro station (Line B) is tastefully appointed with simple furniture. The bright kitchen has all the utensils you need, a stocked refrigerator and a dishwasher.

Apartments U Cisaře

MAP B6 ■ Slezská 898/23, Vinohrady ■ 233 920118 ■ No air conditioning ■ www.hotelsprague.cz/ucisare ■ ⓚ
This booking agency offers six apartments in an 1885 building located a stone's throw from the metro and tram stop Jiřího z Poděbrad, two stops from Wenceslas Square. Fully equipped kitchens, TVs and a basement restaurant help make guests comfortable. The cost includes bed linen and utilities.

Apartments Úvoz

MAP B2 ■ Úvoz 24 ■ 233 920118 ■ No air conditioning ■ www.hotels prague.cz/uvoz ■ ⓚ
Accommodation is in either of two converted art studios in a small Baroque-style house just below the castle. Ideal for those seeking privacy, tranquillity and a romantic setting. The roof terrace has gorgeous views of the city, Petřín Hill and Strahov Monastery.

Apartments Vlašská

MAP B3 ■ Vlašská 7–8 ■ 233 920118 ■ No air conditioning ■ www. hotelsprague.cz/vlasska ■ ⓚ
These five romantic apartments on a palace-lined Malá Strana street have beautiful painted wooden beams, large windows, antique furniture and modern baths and kitchens. Some have balconies or courtyards.

Hunger Wall Residence

MAP C4 ■ Plaská 615/8 ■ 257 404040 ■ No air conditioning ■ www. prague-rentals.com ■ ⓚ
This early 20th-century renovated building, with elements of Art Nouveau architecture, offers 18 stylish and richly furnished apartments each with individual design.

Residence Bene

MAP P3 ■ Dlouhá 48 ■ 222 313171 ■ www. goldencity.cz ■ ⓚ
Situated in the historical heart of Prague, the cosy apartments at Bene are a great alternative to a traditional hotel stay. The Palladium Shopping Centre is a short distance away.

Alchymist Residence Nosticova

MAP D3 ■ Nosticova 1 ■ 257 312513 ■ No air conditioning ■ www. nosticova.com ■ ⓚⓚ
Tucked away in a hidden corner of Malá Strana, the Nosticova is popular with film stars and other VIPs and celebrities. It is located just a few minutes' walk away from Charles Bridge. The apartments are decked out with such fine touches as antique clocks and crystal chandeliers.

Mooo Apartments

MAP E5 ■ Myslíkova 22, Praha 2 ■ 608 278422 ■ www.moooliving.com ■ ⓚⓚ
These stylish and luxurious apartments marry slick urban design with cosy countryside ambience, and are perfect for a design-conscious traveller. They have kitchenettes equipped with the latest Bosch appliances, designer bathrooms, concierge services, high-speed Wi-Fi and some have balconies with magnificent views of the city.

Hotel Residence Řetězová

MAP K5 ■ Řetězová 9 ■ 222 221800 ■ www. residenceretezova.com ■ ⓚⓚⓚ
A palace historically known as the "House at the Three Golden Chains" has been converted into nine spacious apartments. Each has vaulted, decorated or beamed ceilings, wooden floors and Italian baths. The Old Town location makes this the ideal base to explore the surrounding area.

Hotels outside the City Centre

Hotel Anna
MAP B6 ▪ Budečská 17 ▪ 222 513111 ▪ No air conditioning ▪ www. hotelanna.cz ▪ (K)

The Art Nouveau building in a quiet Vinohrady location was built as a private residence at the end of the 19th century. The hotel's 26 rooms are decorated with engravings of historic Prague. The top-floor suites enjoy views of the castle and the Old Town. There's a beautiful breakfast room.

Hotel Belvedere
MAP B5 ▪ Milady Horákové 19, Holešovice ▪ 220 106111 ▪ www. hotelbelvedereprague.cz ▪ (K)

Located near the Trade Fair Palace (Veletržní Palace), the Belvedere is a short walk to the Old Town or Prague Castle. Trams stop just outside. The rooms are very comfortable for the price.

Hotel Excellent
Líbeznická 164/19, Kobylisy ▪ 284 687295 ▪ No air conditioning ▪ www.hotel-excellent.cz ▪ (K)

This small hotel lives up to its name if you don't mind being away from the crowd. Your hosts are happy to book flights, train tickets or seats at the opera, or just show you around town.

Hotel Ibis
Plzeňská 14, Smíchov ▪ 221 701700 ▪ www.ibis. com ▪ (K)

A no-nonsense hotel with modern amenities and a devotion to customer service. Rooms are small and comfortable. This is a good choice for travellers who don't want to spend a lot of time sitting around.

Hotel Vyšehrad
MAP B6 ▪ Marie Cibulkové 29, Vyšehrad ▪ 261 225592 ▪ www. hotel-vysehrad.cz ▪ (K)

Set behind the Congress Centre and close to the monuments of Vyšehrad, this hotel has modern amenities but retains its 19th-century charm.

Pension Karel
Mutěnínská 1119/23, Stodůlky ▪ 235 517563 ▪ www.pension-karel. com ▪ (K)

This small pension in Prague's far-flung western suburbs has simple rooms and a basic breakfast. The owners are very friendly.

Akcent Hotel
MAP A6 ▪ Stroupež-nického 1, Smíchov ▪ 257 003494 ▪ www.akcent-hotel.cz ▪ (K)(K)

This modern three-star hotel has splendid views of Prague from all 53 of its rooms. It is located on the seventh floor of a 1930s Functionalist-style office building.

Dorint Don Giovanni Prague
MAP B6 ▪ Vinohradská 157a, Žižkov ▪ 267 031111 ▪ hotel-prag. dorint.com ▪ (K)(K)

The Don Giovanni offers excellent value in the form of its 356 elegant rooms and 41 suites. Hotel guests can take advantage of the spa treatment facilities and the babysitting service. Conveniently located near

metro, bus and tram stops.

Hotel Diplomat
MAP A5 ▪ Evropská 15, Dejvice ▪ 296 559111 ▪ www.vi-hotels.com/en/ diplomat ▪ (K)(K)

Near, but not within earshot of the airport, the Diplomat has 398 rooms. Facilities include several restaurants, a business centre and an indoor go-cart track. Children under six stay for free. There's good access to the centre.

Hotel Julián
MAP A6 ▪ Elišky Peškové 11, Smíchov ▪ 257 311150 ▪ www.hotel julian.com ▪ (K)(K)

Within walking distance of Malá Strana, the Julián is an Art Nouveau charmer, with red-velvet lift and a fireside library. Some suites have a kitchen and there is a business centre.

Louren Hotel
MAP B6 ▪ Slezská 55, Vinohrady ▪ 224 250025 ▪ www.louren.cz ▪ (K)(K)

Built in 1889, the Louren has had a rocky history, having been damaged in a US bombing raid in 1945 and then nationalized after World War II. Today it is a luxurious hotel with delightful staff.

Hotel Le Palais
MAP B6 ▪ U Zvonařky 1, Vinohrady ▪ 234 634111 ▪ www.palaishotel.cz ▪ (K)(K)(K)

One of Prague's finest examples of *belle époque* architecture, this former residential building from 1841 is now a boutique hotel with plush rooms, a spa and wellness centre and a library. There is also a fine dining restaurant.

For a key to hotel price categories see p140

General Index

Page numbers in **bold**
refer to main entries

A

Aachen, Hans von 14
Absinth 61, 97
Accommodation 139–47
Agnes of Bohemia, St 34, 35, 43
Agnes, Princess 34
Air travel 132, 133
Alchemical symbols 18, 54
Alchemists 61, 63
Alcron 71
Aleš, Mikoláš 19
Altars of Sts Felicissimus and Marcia (The Loreto) 27
Altdorfer, Albrecht, *Martyrdom of St Florian* 35
Anděl Metro Station 51
Anti-Semitism 31
Antiques 76–7, 112
Antonín (artist) 23
Apartments 79, 139, 146–7
Apocalypse Cycle (Dürer) 35
Apostles (Old Town Hall) 20
Arcade (The Loreto) 27
Archbishop's Palace 103
Arras, Matthew d' 16
Art 45
Art Deco (shop) 76
Art Nouveau 19, 36, 37, 58, 85
Josefov 108
New Town 114
Artěl 76
Ashkenazi, Eliezer ben Elijah 31
Astronomical Clock 6, 20, 21, 78, 87
Atheism 61
ATMs 136

B

B&Bs 139, 145–6
Banking 136, 137
Barrandov Studios 126
Bars 74–5
see also Cafés and pubs; Nightlife
Basilica of St James 48, 60, 67, 86, 87

Bassevi, Hendl, grave of 29
Bassevi, Jacob 29
Beer 61, 73, 79
Bell Tower (The Loreto) 26
Beneš, Edvard 15
Bethlehem Square 87
Black Angel's 75
Black light theatre 65, 66, 116
Blue 77, 88
Blue Light Bar 69, 95
Boat trips 65
Bohemia International Folklore Dance Festival 80
Bohemian Chancellery (Old Royal Palace) 14
Bohemian Crown Jewels (St Vitus's Cathedral) 17
Boleslav I the Cruel, Duke of Bohemia 12
Boleslav II, Duke of Bohemia 12
Bonjour, Monsieur Gauguin (Gauguin) 32
Bořivoj I, Duke of Bohemia 12, 42, 100
Botanicus 76, 88
Brahe, Tycho 43, 102
Braun, Matthias 22, 23
Břevnov Monastery 126
Bronzino, Agnolo di Cosimo 102
Brožík, Václav, *The Defenestration of Prague, 23 May 1618* 16
Bruncvík, statue of 23
Budvar 61, 73
Buquoy Palace 96
Bus travel 79, 132, 133

C

Café Slavia 74
Cafés and pubs 74–5, 79
Greater Prague 128
Josefov 113
Malá Strana 98
New Town 120
Old Town 90
Prague Castle and Hradčany 104
restaurants 129
Calvary (Charles Bridge) 22
Čapek, Karel 44
R.U.R. 45

Capuchin Cycle (Convent of St Agnes) 35
Car hire 137
Car travel 133
Caratti, Francesco 96
Casanova, Giacomo 94
Casemates (Vyšehrad) 7, 127
Castles and fortifications
Malá Strana tower 92
Powder Gate 6, 85, 87
Prague Castle 6, 10, **12–15**, 101
Tábor Gate (Vyšehrad) 125, 127
Vyšehrad Castle 61, 123
walls and gates 87
Cathedrals
Cathedral Sts Cyril and Methodius 49, 117
Sts Peter and Paul Cathedral (Vyšehrad) 7, 127
St Vitus Cathedral 10, **16–17**, 48, 64, 101
Cat's Gallery (Kočičí galerie) 77
Celetná 86, 87
Cemeteries
National Cemetery 123
New Jewish Cemetery 126
Old Jewish Cemetery 11, **28–31**, 78, 109
Olšany Cemetery 126
Vyšehrad Cemetery 78
Ceremonial Hall 110
Černý, David, Upside-Down Horse Statue 37, 58
Čertovka (Devil's Canal) 23, 52, 94
České Budějovice 61, 73
Cézanne, Paul, *House in Aix-en-Provence* 32
Chapeau Rouge 75
Chapels
Chapel of the Holy Cross (Prague Castle) 13
Gothic Chapel (Old Town Hall) 20
Mirror Chapel (Clementinum) 67, 86
New Archbishop's Chapel (St Vitus Cathedral) 17

Charles Bridge 10, **22–5**, 93
  itineraries 6, 95
Charles IV, Holy Roman
    Emperor 14, 15, 42
  Hunger Wall 39
  New Town 114
  Our Lady of the Snows 37
  tomb of 16
  Vyšehrad) 127
Charles VI, Holy Roman
    Emperor 31
Children, attractions for 64–7
Chochol, Josef 127
Choco-Story 62
Christmas 81
Churches
  Basilica of St James 48, 60, 67, 86, 87
  Church of the Nativity (The Loreto) 27
  The Loreto 10, **26–7**, 48, 101
  Most Sacred Heart of Our Lord 126
  music recitals 67
  Our Lady before Týn 10, 18, 49, 85
  Our Lady below the Chain 94
  Our Lady of the Snows 37
  Our Lady Victorious 48, 95
  Rotonda of St Martin (Vyšehrad) 125, 127
  St George's Basilica 12, 67
  St Kajetan 67
  St Lawrence 39
  St Ludmila (Vinohrady) 123
  St Martin in the Wall 67
  St Michael 39
  St Nicholas (Malá Strana) 46, 57, 67, 94, 95
  St Nicholas (Old Town) 6, 18, 67, 87
  Sts Simon and Jude 67
  see also Cathedrals;
    Chapels; Monasteries
    and convents
Clementinium 86, 87
Clubs see Nightlife
Coach travel 132, 133
Colloredo-Mansfeld, Count 96

Communism
  Communist Memorial 36
  communist monuments 50–51
  end of 36
  Museum of 51, 117, 118
  rise of 43
Composers 44–5
Concerts
  in churches 67
  free 79
Congress Centre (Vyšehrad) 50, 125, 127
Convent of St Agnes 11, **34–5**, 46, 109
  itineraries 6, 7, 111
  music recitals 67
Counter-Reformation 15, 26
Crystal and glass 76
Cubism
  houses (Vyšehrad) 127
  lamppost 58
Currency 136, 137
Customs regulations 134
Cycling 133
Cyril, St 22
Czech Radio Building 51
Czechoslovakia,
    independence 36, 42

D
Daliborka Tower (Pague Castle) 13
Dance
  clubs 68–9, 89
  festival 80
  venues 66
Dancing House 7, 116, 117
Decorative Arts, Museum of 47
Dee, John 43
The Defenestration of Prague, 23 May 1618 (Brožík) 16
Defenestrations of Prague 14, 15, 116
La Degustation (Bohême Bourgeoise) 70
Delacroix, Eugène, Rider Jaguar Attacking a Horseman 33
Delmedigo, Joseph Solomon 31
Demonstrations, historic 36
Dental care 134, 135
The Devil 55

Devil's Pillar (Vyšehrad) 127
Dientzenhofer, Christoph 94
Dientzenhofer, Kilian Ignac 18, 94
Diet (Old Royal Palace) 14
Dining 138–9
Disabled travellers 135
Discos 68–9, 119
Divaldo Archa 66
Divoka Šárka 59
Don Giovanni (marionette version) 63, 67
Dorotheum 76–7
DOX Centre for Contemporary Art 126
Drahomíra 61
Driving 132, 133, 137
The Drowned Man 60
Dubček, Alexander 37, 43, 51
Dukla Memorial (Old Town Hall) 20
Dům u Minuty 18
Dürer, Albrecht, Apocalypse Cycle 35
Dvořák, Antonín 44, 78, 116
  Dvořák Museum 118
  New World Symphony 45
Dvořák, Karel 22

E
Eccentric Prague 62–3
Electrical appliances 137
Elevator (Old Town Hall) 20
Emaus Devil 61
Emaus Monastery 61, 117
Embassies and consulates 135
Emergencies 134, 135
Erlach, Bernhard Fischer von 27
Erpet Bohemia Crystal 76
Estates Theatre 67
Eufemia, Queen 20

F
False stories 61
Fantova Kavárna 58
Ferdinand I, Holy Roman Emperor 16, 53, 101
Ferdinand II, Holy Roman Emperor 15, 22
Festivals 80–81
Field 71
Film festival 80

La Finestra in Cucina 71, 113
Floods (2002) 94
Food and drink 72–3, 138–9
 see also restaurants
Franciscan Garden 37, 53, 115
Free attractions 78–9
Fuchs, Josef 32
Funicular (Petřín Hill) 39, 93

G

Galleries see Museums and galleries
Gans, David, tombstone of 28, 29
Gargoyles 64, 101
Gauguin, Paul, Bonjour, Monsieur Gauguin 32
Gehry, Frank 116
George of Poděbrady 102
The Golden Key 54
Golden Lane 6, 13, 61, 106–7
Golden Portal (St Vitus Cathedral) 17
The Golden Wheel 54
The Golem 28, 30, 44, 60, 110
Gorazd, Bishop 49
Gorky, Maxim 114
Gothic Cellars (Old Town Hall) 20
Gothic Chapel (Old Town Hall) 20
Gottwald, Klement 50, 125
Grand Café Orient 75
Grand Hotel Evropa 37
Grave symbols (Jewish) 28
Great South Tower (St Vitus Cathedral) 16
Greater Prague 122–9
 cafés and pubs 128
 hotels 147
 map 122–3
 restaurants 129
 sights 123–7
 Three Afternoon Walks 125
Grebovka 59
The Green (Old Town Hall) 20
The Green Lobster 55
Green Wheat (Van Gogh) 32–3
Gregory IX, Pope 34
Grévin Wax Museum 62
Guláš 72
Gutfreund, Otto, Anxiety 32

H

Halušky 73
Hašek, Jaroslav 44
 The Good Soldier Švejk 45
Haunted places 60–61, 63
Havel, Václav 15, 36, 37, 45
 Disturbing the Peace 45
Health 134, 135
Hemingway Bar 75
Heydrich, Reinhard 49
High Altar (St Vitus's Cathedral) 16
High Synagogue 110
Historic Tram No. 91 65
History 42–3
Hitler, Adolf 31
Holešovice 123
Holocaust 31, 43, 108, 111, 126
Homeless people 62
Horse racing 81
Hospitals 134, 135
Hostels 79, 139, 144–5
Hotel International 59
Hotels 139–47
House at the Black Madonna 47
House at the Golden Ring 46
House at the Stone Bell 18, 46
House signs 54–5
Hrabal, Bohumil 45
Hračky 77
Hradčanské náměstí 103
Hradčany see Prague Castle and Hradčany
Hunger Wall 39
Hus, Jan 19, 43, 87
Hussite Wars 15, 16, 42
Hybernia 66
Hynais, Vojtěch 116

I

Ichnusa Botega Bistro 71
Immigration 134
Inner Courtyard (The Loreto) 26
Innocent IV, Pope 34
Insurance 134
Internet 136
The Iron Man 60
Itineraries
 A Day in Hradčany 103
 A Day in the Jewish Quarter 111
 A Day in Malá Strana 95

Itineraries (cont.)
 A Day in the New Town 117
 Four Days in Prague 6–7
 A Stroll around the Old Town 87
 Three Afternoon Walks 125
 Two Days in Prague 6
 see also Trips and tours

J

Jackson, Michael 50
Jaffe, Mordechai ben Abraham 31
Jan Hus Memorial 19
Jazz 69, 89, 119
Jesuits 49, 86, 94
Jewish community 31, 108–11
 Jewish leaders 31
 Old Jewish Cemetery 28–31
 see also Synagogues
Jewish Museum 6, 47, 49
Jewish Town Hall 110, 111
John Lennon Wall 78, 93, 95
John of Luxembourg 14, 18, 21
John of Nepomuk, St 43
 Charles Bridge 22, 61
 statues of 22, 103
 tomb of 17, 46, 48
John Paul II, Pope 34
Josefov 6, 47, **108–13**
 cafés and restaurants 113
 A Day in the Jewish Quarter 111
 map 108–9
 shopping 112
 sights 109–11
Josefov Town Hall 30
Joseph II, Holy Roman Emperor 31, 108

K

Kafka, Franz 18, 19, 31, 43, 44
 The Castle 45
 grave 126
 The Trial 45
Kampa Island 52, 78, 94
Kampa Park 70
Kara, Avigdor, grave 28
Karel Zeman Museum 59
Karlova 86, 87

Karlovo náměstí 117
Karlovy lázně 69, 89
Karlovy Vary International Film Festival 80
Kaunitz Palace 96
Kavárnas 74–5
Kelley, Edward 43
Kepler, Johannes 29, 42, 86
Khrushchev, Nikita 50
Kinský Palace 19, 46
Klaus, Václav 15
Klausen Synagogue 28, 110, 111
Knedlíky 72
Křížík Fountain 63, 124
Krymská 59
Kundera, Milan 45
　The Unbearable Lightness of Being 45

L
Lamppost, Cubist 58
Landau, Yechezkel ben Yehuda 31
Language 159–60
Langweil, Antonín 118
Lapidárium 124, 126
Laterna Magika 66, 116
Laurens, Henri, *Head of a Young Girl* 33
Le Corbusier 32
Lennon, John 61, 78, 93
Letná, view from the 79
Letná Park 124
Letná Plinth 50
Liechtenstein Palace 96
Literature 44–5
Lobkowicz Palace (Prague Castle) 12, 96
Local Artists Praha 77
Loew ben Bezalel, Rabbi Judah 31, 60, 110
　grave of 28
　Old-New Synagogue 30, 44
Loos, Adolf 126
Loretánské náměstí 26
The Loreto 10, **26–7**, 48, 101
Lorraine Cross (Charles Bridge) 22
Louis Wing (Old Royal Palace) 14
Lucerna Music Bar 69, 119
Ludvík II, King of Bohemia 16
Ludwig, Karel 51
Luitgard, St, statue 23
Lunch 79

Luntshits, Ephraim Solomon ben Aaron of 31
Lurago, Anselmo 13
Luxury hotels 140–41

M
McGee's Ghost Tours 63
Mácha, Karel Hynek, statue 39
The Mad Barber 61
Magic Flute (marionette version) 63
Maisel, Mordechai 31, 43, 110
　grave of 28
Maisel Synagogue 110, 111
Malá Strana 6, 7, 92–9, 130–31
　cafés and pubs 98
　A Day in Malá Strana 95
　hotels 142–3
　map 92
　restaurants 99
　shopping 97
　sights 93–4
Malé náměstí 19
Malostranské náměstí 7, 94, 95
Maltézské náměstí 94
Mánes, Galerie 117, 118
Maria Theresa, Empress 14, 54, 102
Marian Column 19
Marionettes, Mozart operas 63
Markets 76–7
Martyrdom of St Florian (Altdorfer) 35
Mary, the Virgin 26, 27, 101
Masaryk, Jan 61
Masaryk, Tomáš Garrigue 15, 31, 32
Masopust 81
Mathey, Jean-Baptiste 126
Matthias, Holy Roman Emperor 42
May Day 80
Mecca 69
Methodius, St 22
Metro 132, 133
Meyrink, Gustav 44
Michna Palace 96
Mikuláš 81
Mikuláš of Kadaň 21
Milunic, Vlado 116
Mirror Chapel (Clementinum) 67, 86

Mirror Maze (Petřín Hill) 39, 64
Mlada, Princess 12
Mobile phones 136
Monasteries and convents
　Břevnov Monastery 126
　Convent of St Agnes 11, **34–5**, 67, 109
　Emaus Monastery 61, 117
　Strahov Monastery 7, 38, 39
Money-saving tips 79
Montanelli Museum 46
Morzin Palace 96
Most Sacred Heart of Our Lord, Church of the 126
Mozart, Wolfgang Amadeus 44, 63, 94
　Estates Theatre 67
　marionette operas 63, 67
Mucha, Alfons 17
　Mucha Museum 118
　Slav Epic 45
Munich Agreement 31, 43
Municipal Gallery 18
Municipal House 6, 85, 87, 102
Museums and galleries 46–7
　Choco-Story 62
　DOX Centre for Contemporary Art 126
　Dvořák Museum 118
　Galerie Mánes 117, 118
　Galerie Rudolfinum 46
　Galerie Via Art 118
　Grévin Wax Museum 62
　Jewish Museum 6, 47, 49
　Karel Zeman Museum 59
　Lapidárium 124, 126
　Lobkowicz Palace (Prague Castle) 12
　Montanelli Museum 46
　Mucha Museum 118
　Municipal Gallery 18
　Museum of Communism 51, 117, 118
　Museum of Decorative Arts 47
　Museum of Torture 62
　Mysteriae Pragensis 60
　National Gallery 6, 7, 11, 19, 32–5, 46
　National Memorial on the Vítkov Hill 50
　National Museum 6, 36, 46, 117, 118

Museums and galleries (cont.)
National Technical Museum 47, 123
New Town 118
Police Museum 118
Postal Museum 118
Prague City Gallery 46
Prague City Museum 118
Public Transport Museum 47
Sex Machines Museum 62–3
Smetana Museum 46
The Story of Prague Castle (Old Royal Palace) 14
Trade Fair Palace 7, 11, **32–3**, 46, 123
Václav Špála Gallery 118
Music 44–5
clubs 68–9, 89
festival 80
tickets 79
venues 66–7
Musicals 63
Můstek 116
Myself, Self Portrait (Rousseau) 33
Mysteriae Pragensis 60

N

Na Příkopě 114
Náměstí Republiky 114
Náplavka 59, 79
Náplavka Farmers' Market 77
Národní třída 6, 7, 116, 117
National Awakening 22
National Cemetery 123
National Gallery 46
Convent of St Agnes 6, 11, **34–5**, 46, 109
Kinský Palace 19, 46
Salm Palace 46
Schwarzenberg Palace 46, 103
Sternberg Palace 46, 102, 103
Trade Fair Palace 7, 11, **32–3**, 46, 123
National holidays 81
National Marionette Theatre 63, 64, 67
National Memorial on the Vítkov Hill 50, 125
National Museum 6, 36, 46, 117, 118
New Building 51

National Technical Museum 47, 123
National Theatre 6, 7, 66, 116, 117
Nazi regime 31, 43, 49, 110
Němcová, Božena, *The Grandmother* 45
Nephele Mound (Old Jewish Cemetery) 28
Neruda, Jan 54, 55, 93
Nerudova 6, 54, 93, 95
New Archbishop's Chapel (St Vitus Cathedral) 17
New Building of the National Museum 51
New Castle Steps 102, 103
New Jewish Cemetery 126
New Town 6, 114–21
cafés and pubs 120
A Day in the New Town 117
hotels 143–4
map 115
nightlife 119
restaurants 121
sights 114–18
New Town Hall 116
Newspapers 136
Nightlife 68–9, 74–5
New Town 119
Old Town 89
Nostitz Palace 96
Novák, V. Karel 50
Novotný bank 40–41
Nový Svět 7, 102, 103
Nusle Bridge 127

O

Observation Tower 38
Off the Beaten Track 58–9
Old Castle Steps 102
Old Jewish Cemetery 11, **28–31**, 78, 109
itineraries 6, 111
Old Land Rolls Room (Old Royal Palace) 14
Old Royal Palace 6, 12, 14–15
Old Town 84–91
cafés and pubs 90
hotels 141–2
map 84–5
nightlife 89
restaurants 91
shopping 88
sights 85–7
A Stroll around the Old Town 87
Old Town Bridge Tower 22

Old Town Hall 18, 20–21, 46, 87
Old Town Square 8–9, 10, **18–21**, 85
itineraries 6, 87
Old-New Synagogue 30, 31, 44, 48, 109
itineraries 111
Olomoucké syrečky 72
Olšany Cemetery 126
One-armed thief 60
Opening hours 136–7
Opera 66, 79
Oppenheim, Rabbi David ben Abraham 31
grave of 29
Ottokar I, King of Bohemia 34
Ottokar II, King of Bohemia 15, 52, 124
Our Lady before Týn 10, 18, 49, 85
Our Lady below the Chain 94
Our Lady of the Mangles 23
Our Lady of the Snows 37
Our Lady Victorious 48, 95

P

Palác Akropolis 68, 124
Palác Koruna 36
Palác Lucerna 36, 37, 58
Palaces
Archbishop's Palace 103
Buquoy Palace 96
Kaunitz Palace 96
Kinský Palace 19, 46
Liechtenstein Palace 96
Lobkowicz Palace (Prague Castle) 12, 96
Malá Strana 96
Michna Palace 96
Morzin Palace 96
Nostitz Palace 96
Old Royal Palace 6, 12, 14–15
Rosenberg Palace (Prague Castle) 13
Salm Palace 46
Schoenborn Palace 96
Schwarzenberg Palace 46, 103
Sternberg Palace 46, 102, 103
Thun-Hohenstein Palace 96
Toskánský Palace 103
Troja Château 46, 124, 125, 126
Wallenstein Palace 96

Palach, Jan 36, 126
Palackého náměstí 117
Palacký, František 117
Pálffy Palác 71, 99
Pardubice Steeplechase 81
Pařížská street 7, 108
Parks and gardens 52–3
   Divoka Šárka 59
   Franciscan Garden 37, 53, 115
   Kampa Island 52, 78, 94
   Letná Park 124
   Petřín Hill 7, 11, **38–9**, 52, 93
   Prague Castle Grounds 78
   Riegrovy sady 59
   Royal Garden (Prague Castle) 53, 101
   South Gardens (Prague Castle) 12, 53
   Střelecký ostrov 53
   Stromkova 7, 52, 124
   Vojanovy sady 52
   Vyšehrad 7, 52
   Wallenstein Garden 7, 52, 79, 95
Parléř, Petr
   Old Royal Palace 14
   Old Town Bridge Tower 22
   St Vitus Cathedral 16, 17
Passes 79
Passports 134, 135
Peak season 79, 139
Pensions 145–6
Performing arts venues 66–7
Personal security 134–5
Perun (pagan god) 38
Petřín Hill 7, 11, **38–9**, 52, 93
Pharmacies 134, 135
Phrase book 159–60
Picasso, Pablo, *Self-Portrait* 33
Pilsner Urquell 73
Pinkas Synagogue 29, 49, 111
Pivní sýr 72
Pivovarský dům 74
Plečnik, Josip 126
Plzeňská restaurace v Obecním domu 71
Pokorny, Karel, *Sbratření* 51
Police 134, 135
Police Museum 118

Ponec 66
Postal Museum 118
Postal services 136
Powder Gate 6, 85, 87
Prague Castle 6, 10, **12–15**, 101, 103
   Grounds 78
Prague Castle and Hradčany 100–107
   cafés and pubs 104
   A Day in Hradčany 103
   hotels 142–3
   map 100–101
   restaurants 105
   sights 101–3
Prague City Gallery 46
Prague City Museum 118
Prague Spring 43, 51
Prague Spring International Music Festival 80, 127
Prague Sun (The Loreto) 27
Prague Writer's Festival 80
Prague Zoo 7, 65, 123, 125
Pragulic 62
Přemyslid dynasty 10, 34, 123
Prices 79, 139
Public Transport Museum 47
Pubs see Bars; Cafés and pubs
Puchner Altarpiece (Convent of St Agnes) 35
Puppet shows 63, 64

R
Radio 136, 137
Radnické schody 103
Radost FX 68, 117, 119
Rail travel 132, 133
Rapoport, Solomon Judah Lieb 31
The Red Lamb 54
Rejt, Benedikt 14
Religion 61
Restaurants 70–71, 138–9
   Greater Prague 129
   Josefov 113
   Malá Strana 99
   New Town 121
   Old Town 91
   Prague Castle and Hradčany 105
Riders' Staircase (Old Royal Palace) 14

Riegrovy sady 59
Říma, Bobeř 60
Road travel 132, 133
Rock Café 69
Rodin, Auguste, *St John the Baptist* 32
Rohlíky 73
Rosenberg Palace (Prague Castle) 13
Rotonda of St Martin (Vyšehrad) 125, 127
Rott House 19
Rousseau, Henri, *Myself, Self Portrait* 33
Roxy 68, 89
Royal Crypt (St Vitus Cathedral) 16
Royal Garden (Prague Castle) 53, 101
Royal Oratory (St Vitus Cathedral) 17
Royal Route 102
Rudolf II, Holy Roman Emperor 31, 42, 102
   St Vitus Cathedral 15
   Stromovka 124
   as werewolf 61
Rudolfinum 46, 66
Rulers 15

S
Safety 134, 135
St George's Basilica 12, 67
St George's Convent 12
St John the Baptist (Rodin) 32
St Kajetan, Church of 67
St Lawrence, Church of 39
St Ludmila, Church of (Vinohrady) 123
St Martin in the Wall, Church of 67
St Michael, Church of 39
St Nicholas's Church (Malá Strana) 46, 57, 67, 94, 95
St Nicholas's Church (Old Town) 6, 18, 67, 87
St Vitus Cathedral 10, **16–17**, 48, 64, 101
   itineraries 6, 103
St Wenceslas's Horse 55
St Wilgefortis Altar (The Loreto) 27
Sts Peter and Paul Cathedral (Vyšehrad) 7, 127

Salm Palace 46
Santa Casa (The Loreto) 26, 27, 101
Santini-Aichel, Giovanni 96
SaSaZu 68
Sbratření (Pokorny) 51
Schoenborn Palace 96
Schwarzenberg Palace 46, 103
Self-Portrait (Picasso) 33
Sex Machines Museum 62–3
Shopping 76–7, 138, 139
  Josefov 112
  Malá Strana 97
  Old Town 88
Sidon, Efraim Karol 31
Sigismund bell (St Vitus Cathedral) 17
Silvestr 81
Škroup, František 111
Slav Epic (Mucha) 45
Slavín Monument (Vyšehrad) 7, 127
Slovaks 61
Smažený sýr 73
Smetana, Bedřich 44, 78, 116, 123
  grave 122, 127
  Smetana Museum 46
  Vltava 45
Smetana Embankment 40–41
Smetana Hall 66
Smíchov 126
Soběslav Residence (Old Royal Palace) 14
Socialist-Realism 59
South Gardens (Prague Castle) 12, 53
Soviet Union 43
Spanish Synagogue 49, 67, 111
Špillar, Karel 85
Stag Moat (Prague Castle) 53, 61, 102
Stalin, Joseph 50, 124
State Opera 66
Štefánik's Observatory 39
Sternberg, Count 126
Sternberg Palace 46, 102, 103
Štorch House 19, 55
The Story of Prague Castle (Old Royal Palace) 14
Strahov Monastery 7, 38, 39
Strahov Stadium 38, 50
Strakonice Madonna 34

Střelecký ostrov 53
Stromkova 7, 52, 124, 125
Sts Cyril and Methodius, Cathedral of 49, 117
Sts Simon and Jude, Church of 67
Sucharda, Vojtěch 20
Svíčková na smetaně 72
Svobodné slovo Balcony 37
Swans, feeding 64, 78
Synagogues
  High Synagogue 110
  Klausen Synagogue 28, 110, 111
  Maisel Synagogue 110
  Old-New Synagogue 30, 31, 44, 48, 109, 111
  Pinkas Synagogue 29, 49, 111
  Spanish Synagogue 49, 67, 111

T

Tábor Gate (Vyšehrad) 125, 127
Táborský, Jan 20, 127
Tartars 87
Taxis 79, 133
Telephone services 136
Television 136
Terasa U Zlaté Studně 71
Terezín concentration camp 31, 111
Theatre 66–7
Theodoricus, Master 34
Thirty Years' War 14, 15, 20, 42, 96
The Three Fiddles 55
The Three Lilies 55
Thun-Hohenstein Palace 96
Tickets
  for music events 79
  public transport 133
Time zone 137
Tipping 139
Torture, Museum of 62
Toulouse-Lautrec, Henri, *At the Moulin Rouge* 33
Tourist information 137
Trade Fair Palace 7, 11, **32–3**, 46, 123
Trams 132–3
Travel 132–3
  safety advice 134, 135
Treasury (The Loreto) 27

Třeboň Altarpiece (Convent of St Agnes) 35
Tretter's 75
Trinitarian Order, Statue of the 23
Trips and tours 138, 139
  see also Itineraries
Troja 124, 125
Troja Château 46, 124, 125, 126
The Two Suns 54
Týl, Oldrich 32

U

U Fleků 74, 120
U Malého Glena 69
U Tří Růží 75
U Zlatého tygra 74
Ungelt 19, 86, 87
  Turk in 60
Upside-Down Horse Statue (Černý) 37, 58
Utopence 72

V

V Zátiší 70
Václav Havel Airport Prague 132, 133
Václav Špála Gallery 118
Van Gogh, Vincent, *Green Wheat* 32–3
Vánoce 81
Velhartice Altarpiece (Convent of St Agnes) 35
Velvet Revolution 34, 37, 43, 127
Vepřoknedlozelo 73
Via Art, Galerie 118
Viewing Gallery (Old Town Hall) 20
Villa Müller 126
Vinohrady 123, 125
Visas 134, 135
Vitus, St 16
Vladislav II 15, 16, 17, 85
Vladislav Hall (Old Royal Palace) 14, 15
Vltava, River 40–41, 53, 78, 82–3
  boat trips 65
Vojanovy sady 52, 95
Vratislav I, Duke of Bohemia 12
Vratislav II, King of Bohemia 127
Vyšehrad 7, 52, 123, 125
  hotels 147
  sights 127

Vyšehrad Castle 61
Vyšehrad Cemetery 78
Vyšší Brod Altarpiece
  (Convent of St Agnes)
  34–5, 109
Výstaviště 7, 65, 124,
  125

W

Walking 133
  free tours 79
  tours 62
Wallenstein, Albrecht von
  43, 52, 96
Wallenstein Garden 7, 52,
  79, 95
Wallenstein Palace 96
Warsaw Pact invasion 43,
  45, 51
Weather 137

Wenceslas I, King (St
  Wenceslas) 13, 15, 16,
  43
  assassination 42
  statues 36, 37, 126
  tomb of 17, 46
Wenceslas IV, King 14,
  15, 16, 20
Wenceslas Square 11,
  36–7, 114
  itineraries 6, 7, 117
Werewolf 61
White Mountain, Battle
  of 15, 20, 42
White Mountain Memorial
  20
The White Swan 54
White Tower (Prague
  Castle) 12, 65
Wilgefortis, St 27

Wine 79
World War I 42
World War II 20, 21, 43,
  117
  Jewish community 31,
  108
Writers 44–5, 80

Z

Zátopek, Emil 43
Zbraslav Madonna 34
Želivský, Jan 36, 114,
  116
Zemach, Mordechai, grave
  29
Zeman, Karel 59
Zeman, Miloš 101
Žižka, Jan 50, 124, 125
Žižkov 79, 124, 125
Žižkov TV Tower 50, 125

Acknowledgments

Author
Theodore Schwinke

Additional contributor
Mark Baker

Publishing Director Georgina Dee

Publisher Vivien Antwi

Design Director Phil Ormerod

Editorial Ankita Awasthi-Tröger, Michelle Crane, Rachel Fox, Priyanka Kumar, Freddie Marriage, Alison McGill, Fíodhna Ní Ghríofa, Scarlett O'Hara, Sally Schafer, Hollie Teague

Cover Design Richard Czapnik

Design Sunita Gahir

Picture Research Susie Peachey, Ellen Root, Lucy Sienkowska, Oran Tarjan

Cartography Subhashree Bharti, Suresh Kumar, Casper Morris

DTP Jason Little

Production Nancy-Jane Maun

Factchecker Filip Polonský

Proofreader Susanne Hillen

Indexer Helen Peters

Illustrator chrisorr.com

First edition created by Sargasso Media Ltd, London

Revisions Team
Marc di Duca, Alice Fewery, Sumita Khatwani, George Nimmo, Vinita Venugopal

Commissioned Photography
Jiri Dolezal, Eddie Gerald, Nigel Hudson, Jiri Kopriva, Vladimir Kozlik, Frantisek Preucil, Rough Guides/Eddie Gerald, Rough Guides/Jon Cunningham, Rough Guides/Natascha Sturny, Stanislav Tereba, Peter Wilson

Picture Credits

The publisher would like to thank the following for their kind permission to reproduce their photographs:

Key: a-above; b-below/bottom; c-centre; f-far; l-left; r-right; t-top

4Corners: SIME/Stefano Cellai 2tl, 8–9.

Alamy Images: AA World Travel Library 119cl; age fotostock/Saturno Dona 51b; Radim Beznoska 42bc, 60c, 81tr; Home Bird 73tr; Petr Bonek 16br; Alena Brozova 14br; David Cole 44tl; David Crausby 20cb; CTK 44bl, /Hajsky Libor 43clb, /Kestner Karel 45tl, /Pavel Vacha 45clb; DPA Picture Alliance/Berliner Verlag /Archiv 43cla; europix 105clb; Mark Eveleigh 55bl; FineArt 44cr, 62bl; Kevin George 97clb; Eddie Gerald 58cr; Hemis.fr /Christophe Boisvieux 15b; Heritage Image Partnership Ltd /Fine Art Images 44br, 45tr; Images & Stories 4crb; Images-Europa 64t; isifa Image Service s.r.o./Landisch 110tc, /Weiss V. 115br; Berger Jiří 38clb; Brenda Kean 102ca; John Kellerman 58bl, 103tl; Yadid Levy 76clb, Loop Images / Anna Stowe 79cl, Ivan Marchuk 28crb; mauritius images GmbH / Cash 36br; Mira 97tr; Stefano Paterna 122tl; PBarchive 15cl; Mo Peerbacus 74br; Pegaz 52t; Prague /Peter Erik Forsberg 43tr, 117cla; PhotoBliss 95bl; J. Pie 53tl, 77b, 105tr; PjrTravel 55br, 86tc; Prisma Archivo 32br; Profimedia.CZ a.s. /Michaela Dusikova 52cr, 59bl, 86cra, 103bl; REDA &CO srl / Federico Meneghetti 30cl; Simon Reddy 72tl; Radomir Rezny 53cr; Shannon99 18cla; Anna Vaczi 73clb; VPC Photo 42tl, 49cr; Terence Waeland 11cra; Mike Withers 63cl.

Ambiente: 99clb, 113tl.

Aromi: 129tl.

Bakeshop Praha: 112tr.

Bohemia Bagel: 98tl.

Bridgeman Images: Narodni Galerie, Prague/*St. Matthew, from*

the chapel of *Karlstejn Castle* (c.1365) Theodoricus of Prague 34bl, / *Resurrection of Christ* (c.1350) Master of the Cycle of Vyssi Brod (tempera on panel) 34–5, /*The Resurrection* (c.1380) Master of the Trebon Altarpiece tempera on panel 35tl, /*Martyrdom of St, Florian* (1516) by Albrecht Altdorfer 35cb; De Agostini Picture Library/A. Dagli Orti 42cra.

Cats Gallery: 77tl.

Český porcelán: Foto Studio H 88bc.

Choco Story Praha: Marek Sustacek 62t.

Corbis: Michele Falzone 49b.

La Degustation: 70cl.

DOX: Jan Slavik 126br.

Dreamstime.com: Abxyz 106–7; Anastasios71 78tl; Andrey Andronov 86b; David Bailey 23cr; Yulia Belousova 93t; Lukas Blazek 37cra; Ryhor Bruyeu 18crb; Neacsu Razvan Chirnoaga 36cla; Cividin 94crb; Sorin Colac 26cl, 54tl, 85tl; Ionut David 38–9, 39cra; Delstudio 19c, 84tl; Dermot68 47cr; Pavel Dospiva 37clb; Dragoneye 6cb; Emicristea 12cla; Frenta 4cla; Marian Garai 127ca, 127br; GoneWithTheWind 3tl, 12crb, 82–3; Gornostaj 2tr, 40–41; Grounder 102b; Nataliya Hora 24–5; Intrepix 36–7; Jakatics 101tl; Julia179 67bl; Kajanek 19tl; Daniel Korzeniewski 85br; Edward Lemery Iii 23bc; Miroslav Liska 16–17; Lurpic99 28–9; Mariell 10ca; Marina99 10clb, 78br; Mikhail Markovskiy 123tl; Ewa Mazur 39crb; Krisztian Miklosy 13crb; Mirekdeml 52b; Martin Molcan 3tr, 12–13, 130–31; Chris Moncrieff 17cr; Peteer 72cra; Ploutarxina 10crb; Pytyczech 10cla; Juha Remes 30b; Radomír Režný 23tl, 37tr, 56–7; Saky13 50clb; Tatiana Savvateeva 87tl; Schvirag 64br; Konstantin Semenov 22bl; Oleksii Sergieiev 87bl; Siloto 17bc; Slowcentury 61tr; Krzysztof Slusarczyk 95tl; Smilingsunray 72b; Radovan Smokon 31br; Igor Stevanovic 1, 39tl, 48cl, 65cra; Alyaksandr Stzhalkouski 16cla, 18bc; Andrey Tarantin 4cl; Tavi79 7cr; Thinkart 110cr; Tomas1111 6cla, 10–11, 21bl, 22–3; Uko_jesita 22br; David Pereiras Villagrá 20cla, 111bl;

Vodickap 92tl; Richard Van Der Woude 11tl, 14tr; Wrangel 55t, 76tr, 81cla; Yuri4u80 125bl; Yykkaa 13clb, 63br.

Field Restaurant: 71cra.

Getty Images: Archive Photos 28cl; Heritage Images 32–3.

Globe Bookstore: 120tl.

Grand Café Orient: Jaroslav Turek 75clb.

Hemingway Bar: 75tr.

Hotel Paris: 91tl.

Hotel U Prince: 90bl.

The ICON Hotel & Lounge : 121crb.

iStockphoto.com: GoneWithTheWindStock 29bl.

John Lennon Pub: 98clb.

Karel Zeman Museum: Libor Svacek 59tl.

King Solomon Restaurant: 113br.

Kogo: Frantisek Ortmann 91bc.

Laterna Magika: Petr Našic Jeseniova 66cr.

Little Whale: 99tr.

Lobkowicz Palace Museum and Café: 12bl,104cr.

Loreto Sanctuary: 26br, 27clb, 27crb, 27bc.

Lucerna Music Bar: 69br.

Mary Evans Picture Library: INTERFOTO/Bildarchiv Hansmann 61cl.

Moser Glassworks: 88cla.

Mysteria Pragensia: 60t.

Národní Muzeum: 46tr, 46cl, 125tl, 126tl.

National Gallery Prague: 32clb, 33cr.

National Technical Museum: 47b.

National Theatre Opera and State Opera: 66tl, 67tl, 116crb.

Nebe Cocktail & Music Bar: 119br.

Ponec: 66bl.

Photo Scala, Florence: Jewish Museum, Prague 47tl.

Prague Spring Festival: Ivan Maly 79tr, 80t.

Radisson SAS Alcron Hotel: 71clb.

Radost FX: 68tl.

Restaurace Pastička: 128br.

Rex Shutterstock: Str / Epa 80crb.

Robert Harding Picture Library:
AGE Fotostock/Walter Bibikow 114cl;
Godong 4clb; Fraser Hall 4t; Henryk
T. Kaiser 11crb; Raimund Kutter
26–7; Martin Moxter 4b; Alexander
Poschel 4cra; Phil Robinson 19br;
Travel Pix 11clb; Kimberly Walker
18–19.

Roxy: 89tr; Marek Podhora 68bl.

SaSaZu, Prague: Adi Gilad 68cr.

Studio Šperk: 112bc.

SuperStock: age fotostock/Christian
Goupi 67tr.

Trade Fair Palace: 11tc.

U Fleků: 74cla, 120cr.

Vagon: 89bl.

Wallenstein Palace: 96clb.

Zatisiclub: 70tr.

Zoo Praha: Petr Hamerni ík 65br.

All other images © Dorling
Kindersley

For further information see:
www.dkimages.com

Cover
Front and spine – **4Corners:**
Michael Breitung

Back – **Alamy Images:** Michael
Brooks

Map Cover
4Corners: Michael Breitung

All other images © Dorling
Kindersley

For further information see:
www.dkimages.com

Penguin
Random
House

Printed and bound in China

First American Edition, 2003
Published in the United States by
DK Publishing, 345 Hudson Street,
New York, New York 10014

Copyright 2003, 2018 © Dorling
Kindersley Limited

A Penguin Random House Company

18 19 20 21 10 9 8 7 6 5 4 3 2 1

**Reprinted with revisions 2005, 2009,
2011, 2013, 2015, 2016, 2018**

Published in the UK by Dorling
Kindersley Limited.

A catalog record for this book is available
from the Library of Congress.

ISSN 1479-344X
ISBN 978 1 4654 6896 3

MIX
Paper from
responsible sources
FSC™ C018179

SPECIAL EDITIONS OF
DK TRAVEL GUIDES

DK Travel Guides can be purchased
in bulk quantities at discounted prices
for use in promotions or as premiums.
We are also able to offer special
editions and personalized jackets,
corporate imprints, and excerpts from
all of our books, tailored specifically to
meet your own needs.

To find out more, please contact:

in the US
specialsales@dk.com

in the UK
travelguides@uk.dk.com

in Canada
specialmarkets@dk.com

in Australia
**penguincorporatesales@
penguinrandomhouse.com.au**

*As a guide to abbreviations in visitor information
blocks:* **Adm** = *admission charge;* **D** = *dinner.*

Phrase Book

In an Emergency

Help!	**Pomoc!**	po-mots
Stop!	**Zastavte!**	zas-tav-te
Call a doctor!	**Zavolejte doktora!**	za-vo-ley-te dok-to-ra!
Call an ambulance!	**Zavolejte sanitku!**	za-vo-ley-te sa-nit-ku!
Call the police!	**Zavolejte policii!**	za-vo-ley-te poli-tsi-yi!
Call the fire brigade!	**Zavolejte hasiče**	za-vo-ley-te ha-si-che
Where is the telephone?	**Kde je telefon?**	gde ye te-le-fohn?
the nearest hospital?	**nejbližší nemocnice?**	ney-blizh-shee ne-mo-tsnyi-tse?

Communication Essentials

Yes/No	**Ano/Ne**	ano/ne
Please	**Prosím**	pro-seem
Thank you	**Děkuji vám**	dye-ku-ji vahm
Excuse me	**Prosím vás**	pro-seem vahs
Hello	**Dobrý den**	do-bree den
Goodbye	**Na shledanou**	na shle-da-nou
Good evening	**Dobrý večer**	do-bree ve-cher
morning	**ráno**	rah-no
afternoon	**odpoledne**	od-po-led-ne
evening	**večer**	ve-cher
yesterday	**včera**	vche-ra
today	**dnes**	dnes
tomorrow	**zítra**	zee-tra
here	**tady**	ta-di
there	**tam**	tam
What?	**Co?**	tso?
When?	**Kdy?**	gdi?
Why?	**Proč?**	proch?
Where?	**Kde?**	gde?

Useful Phrases

How are you?	**Jak se máte?**	yak se mah-te?
Very well, thank you.	**Velmi dobře děkuji**	vel-mi do-brze dye-ku-yi
Pleased to meet you	**Těší mě**	tye-shee mnye
See you soon	**Uvidíme se brzy**	u-vi-dyee-me-se brzy
That's fine	**To je v pořádku**	to ye vpo-rzhahdku
Where is/are…?	**Kde je/jsou …?**	gde ye/ysou …?
How long does it take to get to…?	**Jak dlouho to trvá se dostat do…?**	yak dlou-ho to tr-vah se dos-tat …?
How do I get to…?	**Jak se dostanu k …?**	yak se dos-ta-nuh k…?
Do you speak English?	**Mluvíte anglicky?**	mlu-vee-te an-glits-ki?
I don't understand	**Nerozumím**	ne-ro-zu-meem
Could you speak more slowly?	**Mohl(a)* byste mluvit trochu pomaleji?**	mo-hl(a) bys-te mlu-vit tro-khu po-ma-ley?
Pardon?	**Prosím?**	pro-seem?
I'm lost	**Ztratil(a)* jsem se**	stra-tyil (a) ysem se

Sightseeing

art gallery	**galerie**	ga-le-ri-ye
church	**kostel**	kos-tel
garden	**zahrada**	za-hra-da
library	**knihovna**	knyi-hov-na
museum	**muzeum**	mu-ze-um
railway station	**nádraží**	nah-dra-zhee
tourist information	**turistické informace**	tu-ris-tits-ke in-for-ma-tse
closed for the public holiday	**státní svátek**	staht-nyee svah-tek

Shopping

How much does this cost?	**Co to stojí?**	tso to sto-yee?
I would like…	**Chtěl(a)* bych…**	khtyel(a) bikh…
Do you have…?	**Máte…?**	maa-te …?
I'm just looking	**Jenom se dívám**	ye-nom se dyee-vahm
Do you take credit cards?	**Berete kreditní karty?**	be-re-te kre-dit –nyee kar-ti?
What time do you open/close?	**V kolik otevíráte/ zavíráte?**	v ko-lik o-te-vee-rah-te/ za-vee-rah-te?
this one	**tento**	ten-to
that one	**tamten**	tam-ten
expensive	**drahý**	dra-hee
cheap	**levný**	lev-nee
size	**velikost**	ve-li-kost
white	**bílý**	bee-lee
black	**černý**	cher-nee
red	**červený**	cher-ve-nee
yellow	**žlutý**	zhlu-tee
green	**zelený**	ze-le-nee
blue	**modrý**	mod-ree
brown	**hnědý**	hnye-dee

Types of Shop

bank	**banka**	ban-ka
bakery	**pekárna**	pe-kahr-na
butcher	**řeznictví**	rzhez-nyits-tvee
chemist (prescriptions etc)	**lékárna**	leh-kahr-na
chemist (toiletries etc)	**drogerie**	dro-ge-riye
delicatessen	**lahůdky**	la-hood-ki
grocery	**potraviny**	po-tra-vi-ni
glass	**sklo**	sklo
market	**trh**	trh
post office	**pošta**	posh-ta
supermarket	**samoobsluha**	sa-mo-ob-slu-ha
travel agency	**cestovní kancelář**	tses-tov-nyi kan-tse-laarzh

Staying in a Hotel

Do you have a vacant room?	**Máte volný pokoj?**	mah-te vol-nee po-koy?
double room	**dvoulůžkový pokoj**	dvou-loozh-ko-vee po-koy
with double bed	**s dvojitou postelí**	s dvoy-tou pos-te-lee
twin room	**pokoj s dvěma postelemi**	po-koy sdvye-ma pos-te-le-mi
porter	**vrátný**	vrah-tnee
I have a reservation	**Mám reservaci**	mahm re-zer-va-tsi

alternatives for a female speaker are shown in brackets

Eating Out

Have you got a table for…?	Máte stůl pro …?	mah-te stool pro …?
I'd like to reserve a table	Chtěl(a)* bych rezervovat stůl	khtyel(a) bikh re-zer-vo-vat stool
breakfast	snídaně	snyee-danye
lunch	oběd	ob-yed
dinner	večeře	ve-che-rzhe
The bill, please	Prosím, účet	pro-seem oo-chet
I am a vegetarian	Jsem vegetarián (ka)*	ysem veghe-tariahn(ka)
waitress!	slečno	slech-no
waiter!	pane vrchní!	pane vrkh-nyee!
fixed-price menu	standardní menu	stan-dard-nyee menu
dish of the day	nabídka dne	na-beed-ka dne
starter	předkrm	przhed-krm
main course	hlavní jídlo	hlav-nyee yeed-lo
vegetables	zelenina	ze-le-nyi-na
dessert	zákusek	zah-kusek
cover charge	poplatek	pop-la-tek
wine list	nápojový lístek	nah-po-yo-vee lees-tek
rare (steak)	krvavý	kr-va-vee
medium	středně udělaný	strzhed-nye u-dye-la-nee
well done	dobře udělaný	dobrzhe-u-dye-la-nee
glass	sklenice	sklen-yitse
bottle	láhev	lah-hev
knife	nůž	noozh
fork	vidlička	vid-lich-ka
spoon	lžíce	lzhee-tse

Menu Decoder

biftek	bif-tek	steak
bílé víno	bee-leh ve-no	white wine
bramborové knedlíky	bram-bo-ro-veh kne-dleeki	potato dumplings
brambory	bram-bo-ri	potatoes
chléb	khlehb	bread
cukr	tsukr	sugar
čaj	chay	tea
červené víno	cher-ven-eh vee-no	red wine
grilované	gril-ov-a-neh	grilled
houskové knedlíky	ho-sko-veh kne-dleeki	bread dumplings
hovězí	hov-ye-zee	beef
hranolky	hra-nol-ki	chips
husa	hu-sa	goose
jehněčí	ye-hnye-chee	lamb
kachna	kakh-na	duck
kapr	ka-pr	carp
káva	kah-va	coffee
kuře	ku-rzhe	chicken
kyselé zelí	kis-el-eh zel-ee	sauerkraut
maso	ma-so	meat
máslo	mah-slo	butter
mléko	mleh-ko	milk
mořská jídla	morzh-skah yeed-la	seafood
párek	paa-rek	sausage
pečeny	petsh-en-eh	baked
pečené	pech-en-eh	roast

polévka	po-lehv-ka	soup
pivo	pi-vo	beer
ryba	ri-ba	fish
rýže	ree-zhe	rice
salát	sa-laat/sa-laht	salad
sůl	sool	salt
sýr	seer	cheese
šunka	shun-ka	ham
vařená/ uzená	va-rzhe-nah u-zenah	cooked smoked
telecí	te-le-tsee	veal
vajíčko	va-yeech-ko	egg
vařené	va-rzhe-neh	boiled
vepřové	vep-rzho-veh	pork
voda	vo-da	water
zelenina	ze-le-nyi-na	vegetables

Numbers

1	jedna	yed-na
2	dvě	dvye
3	tř	trzhi
4	čtyři	chti-rzhi
5	pět	pyet
6	šest	shest
7	sedm	sedm
8	osm	osm
9	devět	dev-yet
10	deset	de-set
11	jedenáct	ye-de-nahtst
12	dvanáct	dva-nahtst
13	třináct	trzhi-nahtst
14	čtrnáct	chtr-nahtst
15	patnáct	pat-nahtst
16	šestnáct	shest-nahtst
17	sedmnáct	sedm-nahtst
18	osmnáct	osm-nahtst
19	devatenáct	de-va-te-nahtst
20	dvacet	dva-tset
21	dvacet jedna	dva-tset yed-na
22	dvacet dva	dva-tset dva
30	třicet	trzhi-tset
40	čtyřicet	chti-rzhi-tset
50	padesát	pa-de-saht
60	šedesát	she-de-saht
70	sedmdesát	sedm-de-saht
80	osmdesát	osm-de-saht
90	devadesát	de-va-de-saht
100	sto	sto
1,000	tisíc	tyi-seets
2,000	dva tisíce	dva tyi-see-tse
5,000	pět tisíc	pyet tyi-seets
1,000,000	milión	mi-li-ohn

Time

one minute	jedna minuta	yed-na mi-nu-ta
one hour	jedna hodina	yed-na ho-dyi-na
half an hour	půl hodiny	pool ho-dyi-ni
day	den	den
week	týden	tee-den
Monday	pondělí	pon-dye-lee
Tuesday	úterý	oo-te-ree
Wednesday	středa	strzhe-da
Thursday	čtvrtek	chtvr-tek
Friday	pátek	pah-tek
Saturday	sobota	so-bo-ta
Sunday	neděle	ned-yel-e

*alternatives for a female speaker are shown in brackets